ACHIEVING POSITIVE BEHAVIOUR
A Practical Guide

Patricia Dwyer

Centre for Education Services
Marino Institute
Griffith Avenue
Dublin 9
Ireland

Coláiste Mhuire

MARINO

INSTITUTE OF EDUCATION

Achieving Positive Behaviour
A Practical Guide

First Published 2003 by
Centre for Education Services
Marino Institute
Griffith Avenue
Dublin 9
Ireland

Printing and Layout
by
Typeform Repro

ISBN 1-89916224-2

Achieving Positive Behaviour
A Practical Guide

Publishers Note

The Centre for Education Services at Marino Institute is proud to publish this most significant and practical resource for school communities. The Centre commissioned this work in order to respond to the clear challenges that face schools in relation to behaviour. The many who have been involved in this publication have been acknowledged elsewhere, nonetheless, the Centre at Marino would in a particular way wish to salute Patricia Dwyer for her exhaustive, professional, insightful and eminently practical work. Her long experience in school, as well as her research and presentation skills, have combined to produce this invaluable guide.

This publication represents the fifth in a series that the Centre for Education Services is publishing examining major educational issues in Ireland. The Centre is proud to record its thanks to the Irish Christian Brothers who, through the Marino Trust Fund, have supported this project.

Luke Monahan

Head, Centre for Education Services, Marino Institute

Coláiste Mhuire

MARINO

INSTITUTE OF EDUCATION

ACKNOWLEDGEMENTS

My thanks go to all of the students, teachers and principals who contributed to this work. They shared their views, experiences and good ideas unselfishly and enthusiastically. I would like to thank Luke Monahan for always supporting the work in a positive and creative way and for allowing me to lead the project. My thanks to Brian Flannery and Ferdia Kelly, who with Luke Monahan formed the Behaviour Management Project Steering Committee, for their support and encouragement. A word of thanks is also extended to other members of the Christian Brothers Education Offices, Br. Pat Madigan, Helen O'Brien and Frank Smith, as well as Br. Donal Leader of Marino Institute for their interest in and promotion of the work. This work would not have taken place without the support of the **Marino Trust Fund**, set up by the Irish Christian Brothers. I extend my gratitude to them for being willing to meet the needs of schools in a practical, resourceful way. Special mention to all the staff in the Centre for Education Services for their ongoing backing, in particular Seamus O'Brien for his proofing skills. My thanks go to two friends and former teaching colleagues Vivienne Dunne and Gillian Lonergan for their support and suggestions, and to former colleagues at the Centre, Don Herron and Libby Walsh, for their advice and guidance. I wish to acknowledge the work of Mary Glynn and in particular Miriam Lambe of Marino Institute library. They were able to source the materials I needed and put the most up-to-date books and articles my way. I also extend my thanks to Dr. Maeve Martin, whose knowledge and advice were always only an e-mail away and to Dr. Sinead Breathnach of SDPI for her willingness to allow resources developed by her team to be adapted for use in this work. I would like to acknowledge the work of three American teachers, Colleen Gallagher, Shelli Temple, Lori-Ann Willey. They allowed me to adapt many of their good ideas for classroom management to an Irish context. The work of the Centre is made possible by a terrific administrative team of Maureen McDonagh, Jocelyn McRory and Mai Ralph. I would like to thank them and in particular Ger Carberry of **iapce** for their friendship and support. A big thank you to my family, particularly my husband Ger and the extended Williams clan, and my friends Noel Mooney, Anne Byrne and John Kelly, and to Mary & John Duggan. Without their flexibility and support the visits to schools around the country could not have taken place. Finally, I would like to thank the students and staff of Marino College, from whom I learnt so much about being positive. This book is dedicated to my late parents, Kevin and Phil, whose unfailing belief in the power of education was a priceless legacy, and to Sophie – that she will always love learning.

Table of Contents

SECTION SIX

SECTION SEVEN

SECTION EIGHT

INTRODUCTION

This resource pack has been developed from the work of the Christian Brothers Behaviour Management Project, based in the Centre for Education Services at Marino Institute. Over the past fifteen months desk and field research have been carried out looking at behaviour management in a changing context. The pack is designed to enable schools to review current practices, to analyse what is working well and not so well and to develop Codes of Behaviour which focus on positive behaviour and self-responsibility. While much of the research is based on and informed by Christian Brothers schools it is not exclusively so. The process model and examples of good practice outlined in the pack could be used by any school.

Section One sets out the rationale of the project and gives a brief description of the initial work.

Section Two sets the issue of behaviour management in context, looking at the theory associated with why some schools successfully encourage student responsibility for their own behaviour while others, often similar in make-up and background are unsuccessful.

Section Three presents some of the global responses to behaviour management, with outlines of some of the most frequently used systems.

Section Four describes the work of the project in the Irish context over the past 15 months, focusing on the common themes and good practices encountered as well as the issues of concern raised in the schools visited. It provides information sheets and examples dealing with what is working well in Irish schools.

Section Five outlines a process model designed to move schools from policy to practice and describes several case studies based on the field research. It also offers examples of where policy jumped to practice with no process in between and highlights how policies derived in such a way can prove difficult to implement and sustain.

Section Six supplies samples of audit materials to illustrate the process. These can be adapted to suit any school context. Also contained in this section is some reaction to using the different audit techniques gleaned from participants in the process.

Section Seven recognises that schools are often pressure points with time the most sought after resource of all. Good intentions around developing resources which emphasise positive behaviour may be lost in the day to day rush of school life. This section offers examples and templates of useful resources, an idea bank which can be added to as the school engages in its own process of developing a suitable behaviour code.

Section Eight provides a useful bibliography which may be used to further understand and address the complex issue that is behaviour management.

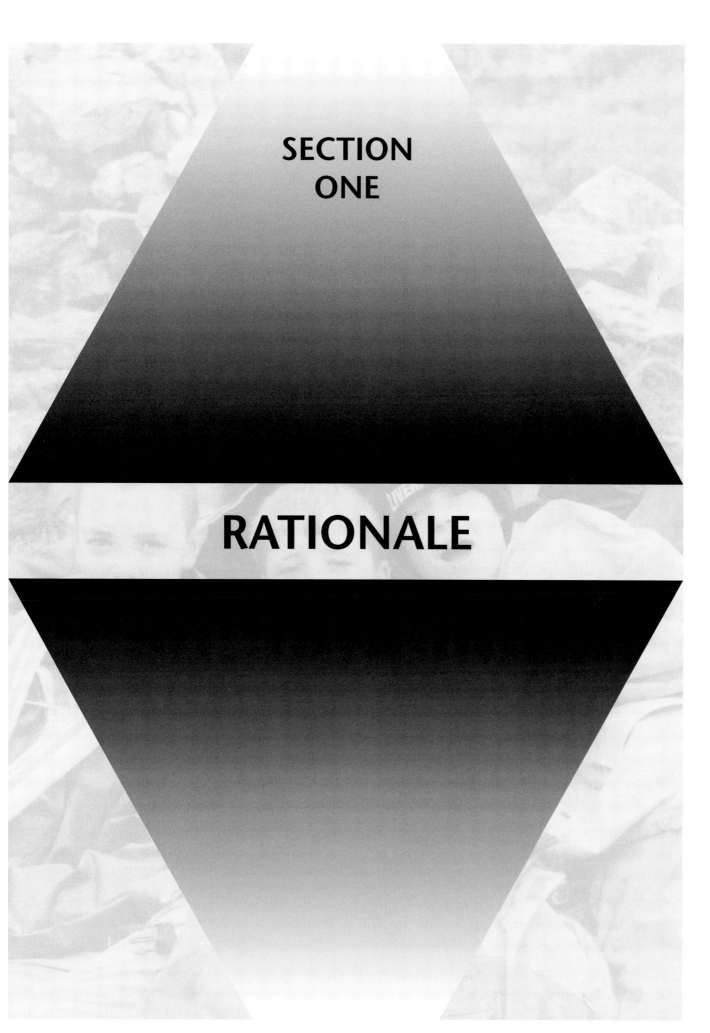

SECTION
ONE

RATIONALE

RATIONALE FOR PROJECT

Introduction

There is no simple formula for creating a whole-school behaviour management system. However, a number of important components have been identified by researchers and practitioners. The process will vary from context to context, hopefully resulting in a plan specific and suitable to each individual school. It will be important, however, that teachers in particular do not perceive the process to be contributing to the sense of 'overload' in schools. The purpose of this resource is to provide stimulus for schools already engaged or about to engage in modifying or developing their own school behaviour code, either as part of the School Plan or as a stand alone document.

To that end it is hoped that the work of this project will help schools to:

- Understand the factors within school which contribute to the way pupils behave

- Be aware of the many factors outside school which can influence student behaviour

- Be aware of the variety of positive behaviour management systems available

- Review as a whole-school community current approaches to dealing with behaviour

- Identify strengths and weaknesses in current practices

- Plan and implement for the future

- Write up those agreed changes in the behaviour code under an overall policy within the School Development Planning Initiative framework

The importance of creating a whole-school policy which succeeds in affording all of our students a chance to improve behaviour and become an important member of the school community cannot be overstated. We need to recognise that students who are not participating fully because of disruptive behaviour, withdrawal from school activities, suspension or exclusion are at risk. Positively managing behaviour requires a range of provisions, from positive prevention for the majority of students to intensive intervention for disruptive, disaffected or vulnerable students. Where students cannot achieve success under the whole school policy we need to consider individual behaviour management plans, individual

education plans and other strategies to ensure their continued participation in the education system.

This project has developed from the recognition that society and students are changing, and that there is a need for a more holistic approach to behaviour management. It has its origins in the Christian Brothers Network of schools. The findings of the Christian Brothers Identity Project, undertaken by the Centre for Education Services and the Christian Brothers Education Offices, highlighted positive, enabling discipline as one of the core components of a Christian Brothers school, as it is in many schools. Some of the key recommendations of that project provide the cornerstone for the work undertaken around behaviour, namely that:

- there is a need to create communities of care where affirmation and encouragement characterise the relationships throughout each school community

- there is a need to acknowledge that good personal relationships form the foundation stone of fair and effective discipline in schools

- there is a need to recognise the importance of multiple intelligence research and pastoral care programmes in the holistic development of students

- models of best practice should be documented, designed & distributed throughout the network

- there is a need to promote, develop, implement & review each school's behaviour policy

The experiences and practices of those schools involved in the initial research indicate the futility of a 'one size fits all' approach to developing a behaviour management strategy. Each school must cater for the needs of its community members in the context in which it operates. The rationale of emphasising a process as well as introducing a policy is that the context in which each school operates will be different. Indeed the perceptions of what constitutes good or positive behaviour will vary from school to school. Therefore a universal "magic potion" handed down from the Christian Brothers education offices, from Marino Institute of Education or from the Department of Education and Science will be ineffective. Given that there are so many causes and manifestations of behavioural problems in schools we must acknowledge what Munn *et al* (1992, p.4) call the "futility of the quest for a universal answer or magic recipes to deal with discipline problems". If we were to ask ten different teachers even in the same school what they define as misbehaviour, we would probably get ten different answers. Go to ten different schools and the definitions would be even further apart. Certainly, what is appropriate in one school will not necessarily be appropriate in another. There is plenty of "agreement that what counts as effective discipline is heavily dependent on the context in which the teacher is operating. The age and the stage of the pupils, the time of the day, the time of year, the content of the lesson and many other factors can all have an influence". Munn *et al.* (1992, p.3)

Research Phase

It was decided in the initial stages to visit a range of schools, mainly though not exclusively in the Christian Brother Network. These visits had several objectives. They allowed the researcher to get a sense of current practices in various schools, primary and post-primary, and to discuss the successes and concerns which those schools were experiencing in the area of behaviour management. They also allowed for the creation of links with people in schools recognised as having good practice. The visits formed an initial framework on how a process might be developed, a process whereby all members of the school community and all stakeholders in the school might be involved in developing and implementing a whole-school behaviour policy. The importance of having in-school people at the core of developing policy cannot be over-emphasised. In Birmingham a major study into positive behaviour has been conducted and the programme introduced. There is clear evidence that a key person or working group from within the staff should take responsibility for auditing the current practices and facilitating the process, possibly with the help of an outside 'critical friend'.

Meetings have been conducted with Principals, Deputy Principals, Year Heads, Class/Form teachers, Learning Support staff and Resource teachers, indeed any member of a school staff who has an interest in the area of behaviour. The involvement of such a wide range of professionals; from primary and post-primary, North and South, indicates the level of interest in the issue and the willingness of schools to share experiences and good practice. Discussions with students have also taken place, an essential aspect of a project which aims to foster positive behaviour and encourage student self-responsibility. Research into good practice has also been expanded to take in ideas from non-Christian Brothers schools who have developed, or are in the process of developing whole-school behaviour policies with a positive emphasis. Visits to education centres in London and Bristol, as well as the St. John Centre, Glasnevin and the Learning Resource Unit, CBS Glen Road, Belfast, have also informed the work of the project.

Having completed the initial research and identified what might work to turn process into policy, a range of audit materials and services were designed and offered to schools in the Christian Brothers network. A number of schools have since engaged in a pilot programme, starting with a review of their current practices around discipline, moving through to the development of new Codes of Behaviour which have been designed in partnership with all members of the school community. Other schools have benefited from the project by accessing resources or availing of staff development at whole staff or working group level.

Subsequent sections of this resource pack include topics for further discussion about behaviour as well as evidence of what schools in our own system and outside Ireland are doing to encourage positive behaviour. Key questions are dispersed throughout the pack to act as prompts for further reflection by school leaders, individual teachers and whole staffs. It also offers a model of a process which can help schools design behaviour policies that aim to prevent the majority of misbehaviour or at least deal with it in a caring and creative way, in true reflection of the tradition of Edmund Rice. Most importantly the handbook emphasises process and its importance at a time when policy is to the forefront for educators working under the impact of legislation. It suggests that process and policy can live together harmoniously and that the pursuit of one can lead to the other taking hold in a more meaningful way. The notion of process is essential since it is in working through that process that we can answer the questions which will be the basis for our policy. In order for the answers to those questions to have real meaning for the life of the school and for the policy which develops from them to bring about the desired changes all stakeholders must be involved.

In essence the process must encourage us to answer the following questions:

- What behaviours do we think can be managed in the classroom?
- What behaviours do we think will require the use of consequences or sanctions?
- What behaviours will have to be dealt with by more senior staff?
- What steps should we include in a 'ladder of referral'?
- What do we expect senior staff to do when we refer problems on to them?
- How can we continue to involve the 'referring' teacher in a useful way so that it is perceived that they are taking problems to the next level in the procedures rather than passing on responsibility?
- How do we intervene with very serious difficulties?
- What ways will we encourage positive behaviour?
- How will we acknowledge the majority of students who do behave?
- How will we be consistent?
- How can we set targets which are identifiable and achievable?
- How will we measure the effectiveness of any changes?
- Do we have a clear timetable written into the process which will allow for evaluation and further recommendations or changes to be made?
- How do we as a school community decide on a common approach?
- How will we involve students and parents?

I am very grateful to the schools listed below, to the Principals, Deputy Principals, teaching staff and students who shared their insights on behaviour management and who were so generous with their time.

- Abbey CBS, Tipperary Town
- Abbey Grammar School, Newry
- CBS Enniscorthy
- CBS Kilkenny
- CBS Primary, Francis Street
- CBS Roscommon
- Coláiste Choilm CBS, Swords
- Coláiste Mhuire, Mullingar
- Coláiste Phadraig, Lucan
- Meanscoil Iognáid Rís, Naas
- Mount Sion Primary School, Waterford.
- Nagle Rice Secondary, Doneraile, Cork
- O'Connell's Primary School, North Richmond Street
- Rice College, Westport, Co. Mayo
- Scoil Mhuire, CBS Primary, Mullingar
- St. Aidan's Primary, Whiterock Road, Belfast
- St. David's CBS, Artane
- St. Joseph's, Sunday's Gate, Drogheda
- St. Laurence O'Toole's Primary School, Seville Place, Dublin 1.
- St. Mary's Academy, Carlow
- St. Mary's Holy Faith Secondary School, Haddington Road, Dublin 4.
- St. Mary's CBS Grammar School, Glen Road, Belfast.
- St. Mary's Senior Primary School, Rowlagh, Dublin 22.
- St. Michael's CB Primary School, Inchicore, Dublin 8.
- St. Paul's CBS, Brunswick Street
- St. Vincent's CBS Secondary School, Glasnevin, Dublin 11

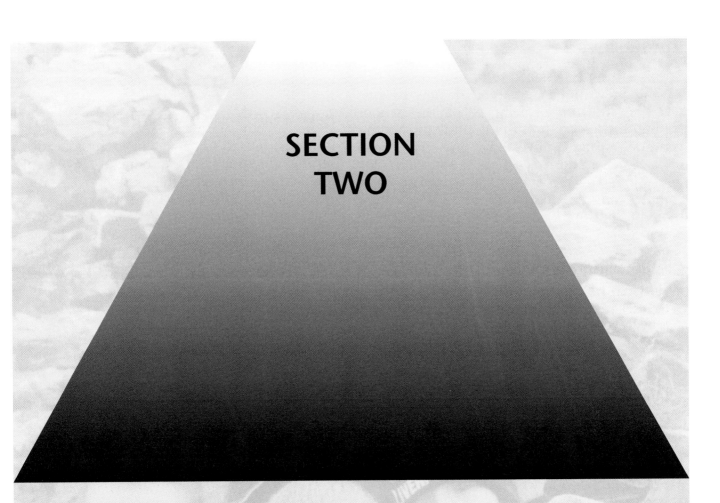

SECTION
TWO

FROM THEORY TO PRACTICE

Introduction

This section is designed to be both descriptive and prescriptive in nature. It aims to give teachers and other members of the school community access to current thinking on the various issues involved in behaviour management and to act as a stimulus for discussion. The recognition that the issue is a complex one emphasises the need for a fully thought out process before any policy is designed.

Challenging behaviours in school – a question of context

> Schools have their own histories, their particular combinations of staff and pupils, their own cultures and circumstances which conspire to produce their particular approaches to discipline policy and practice.
>
> *Munn et al. (1992, p.4)*

Schools today have highly challenging pupils although the degree of indiscipline and the definition of challenging varies greatly depending on the context in which the school operates. The school often appears to be the forum in which students vent their feelings about issues that belong outside of its walls. Yet the school has to deal with these issues and the indiscipline and disaffection they cause in a manner that will have positive outcomes for all students. To understand what "highly challenging" behaviour is we need to look at the nature of misbehaviour. Misbehaviour can range from inattention in class and failure to concentrate to verbal attacks and physical violence. What is deemed "highly challenging" in one school might be a mere misdemeanour, all but ignored, in another. Students often see misbehaviour such as talking in class, chewing gum or running on a corridor as very minor when compared with what they see in everyday life outside the school walls. Drug and alcohol abuse, teen pregnancy and robbery may be just some of the social factors with which they have to live. It is important, therefore, that the school is aware of the existence of such factors in the lives of some, or perhaps all, of their student intake. Yet not all students who come from difficult home scenarios or who have learning difficulties act out. Some schools, irrespective of pupil intake or location in a socio-economically deprived area, successfully manage pupil behaviour so that each pupil feels valued and able to succeed. Concentration on improving those factors we can influence in school can have huge bearing on improving behaviour.

Factors influencing behaviour

Problems related to behaviour in an educational setting are usually the product of a complex interaction between the individual, school, family, community and wider society. The factors that cause students to act out in whatever manner may be categorised broadly in terms of what Watkins and Wagner (1991) call personal, institutional and cultural aspects. The key issues include:

- changes in society;
- family breakdown;
- the role of parents;
- pupil participation and retention rates;
- the culture of schools;
- teacher education;
- school curricula;
- the examinations points system.

Martin (1997, p.8)

Behavioural challenges in our schools include:

- General lack of discipline
- Increasing school violence
- Inefficient use or loss of instructional time
- Over-reliance on punishment based exclusionary strategies (office referrals, detention, out of class exclusions, standing outside classroom door, suspension & expulsion)

The list of poor behaviour experienced on a regular basis is by no means exhaustive but can include those listed in Table 1.

Each of the types of behaviour results in escalating stress for the teacher engaged in trying to manage a classroom. It can prove useful to keep in mind the possible causes (Table 2).

Schools and teachers cannot alleviate the ills of society. However, they can look at the institutional or school related factors involved in designing constructive models of behaviour management. They also need to be more aware of the common characteristics and motivations of students who present with poor behaviour. By doing so they can successfully keep their students adjusted to the dominant culture of the school and focused on learning rather than on railing against authority.

Table1		
DISRUPTION	AGGRESSION	DEFIANCE
Talking out of turn	Answering back	Ignoring a reasonable request
Lack of equipment	Swearing	Silent non-co-operation
Moving out of seat	Leaving the room without permission	Insolence
Playing with objects	Slamming the door	Refusing to undertake a task
Making noises or smells	Banging desks/furniture	
Disturbing others	Threatening violence	
Defacing other people's work	Violence	
Borrowing without permission	Towards another pupil	
Eating in class	Towards the school environment	
Bickering	Towards a member of staff	

Table2	
Common Characteristics of Disruptive Students	Motivation For Disruptive Students
View themselves as failures	Attention
Pessimistic about the future	Power
Lack the confidence to take a chance	Revenge
Have been humiliated frequently	Avoidance of failure
Low self esteem	
Lack of respect for authority figures	

Organisational Issues

Given that almost all children start their school careers eager to please and responsive to learning, it's clear that for a significant minority of students, something happens as they progress through the system to discourage them and throw them off track.

Klein (1999, p.149)

There are many aspects of the ways in which schools organise themselves that militate against good behaviour by all students. They include the curriculum and methodology employed in teaching and learning, the use of resources and the availability of extra-curricular activities that allow non-academic students to shine and to have a role in the culture of the school. Kavanagh (1993, p.67) refers to the problem of curriculum, acknowledging that "the narrow and academic focus of curriculum in most schools along with a highly competitive examination system can exacerbate the 'counter-culture' syndrome unless schools are sensitive to the problem. Among the main ways in which the organisation of schools acts as a barrier to full participation for all students are the following:

- a narrow curriculum which has little of interest for those students who do not come from the traditional middle class family
- standardised tests which examine a pupil's ability in linguistic and numeracy skills rather than any of the other intelligences he or she might possess
- streaming, where students are often separated from their peers based on their performance in an entrance test on one particular morning, or where placement into a particular class group is based on perceived ability
- a rigid timetable where school must begin at nine and end at four (or whichever variation of that schedule suits the administration)

Each of these factors, and others, serve to make some students become more disenchanted and disaffected. There are students who cannot do well on standardised tests, who find themselves in the lowest stream, who do not relate to the material they are supposed to regurgitate in an exam, and who find it extremely difficult to be in school at 9 o'clock. These students are likely to find that school is meaningless in their lives and that codes of behaviour do nothing but emphasise their weaknesses and failures.

The quality of a school's curriculum, interpersonal relationships and organisation directly influence behaviour. The school community must be involved through collaborative school development planning and review processes. A school's code of behaviour reflects the values of the local community within which the school operates. The factors which influence behaviour may include:

- classroom size, shape & location

- student age
- subject taught
- classroom arrangement
- teacher preferences & levels of tolerance
- school environment
- community values
- school guidelines
- Department of Education guidelines

O'Flynn and Kennedy (2000, p.116) outline what students found unpleasant about school:

- being expected to maintain total silence for long periods of time
- reading, especially being asked to read aloud, which they frequently found embarrassing
- the whole class being blamed for a few and subsequently being punished as a group
- not getting a chance to give their point of view
- being very bored for much of their time in school
- not being able to understand the materials being taught
- living under threat of (inevitable) punishment
- giving incorrect responses to teachers' questions and being shown up in front of the whole class
- getting too much homework, not having it done and not knowing how to do it
- being mocked by other students
- being bullied all the time by their own peers. Constant pressure to conform to the group
- feeling uncared for, by the teachers and the school system generally

Professional development in the areas of classroom management and multiple intelligences will alleviate some of these problems perceived by pupils.

School climate and ethos

> Humanity in a school, from headteacher to lunchtime supervisors, from classroom teachers to governors, should be as integral to a school as bricks and mortar.
>
> *Klein (1999, Introduction xvii)*

We have to acknowledge that the influence of the outer environment is stronger than that of the school. However, that is not to say that we should not try to instil in our students a sense of belonging and a feeling that they have a place in the school community. No matter what form a discipline code takes, "the policy of itself is sterile unless it is situated in a school culture which enables the spirit of the policy to be expressed in a positive manner. Such a culture seeks to put each student's total welfare at the heart of all the school endeavours" Kavanagh (1993, p.69). The climate of a school is made up of many elements. It is a product of the relationships between the members of the school community. It includes factors such as the academic climate, teacher expectations of the student population, discipline and homework policies, whether or not there is a strong culture of pastoral care etc. The climate of the school also manifests itself in the rituals and traditions in which the school participates. It includes how success is measured and how success is acknowledged. It exists in tandem with the organisational structures of the school to leave students, teachers and parents with a clear view of whether or not they are valued in the school community. We need to acknowledge that "school climate can be a positive influence on the health of the learning environment or a significant barrier to learning". (Freiberg, 1998, p.22) Such acknowledgement of the huge importance of creating a positive school climate for all, irrespective of class, is essential since there is "substantial evidence that changing school climate and involving parents on a School planning and Management team will substantially raise not only the achievement of low-income, at-risk children but will change their self-concepts and motivation as well". (Haberman, 1991, p.33)

Nowhere is this need for school climate to be positive more acute than in the area of behaviour management where we are trying to teach students lessons that will remain long after they have forgotten algebra or geography. The ethos of the school and the relationships created within that ethos are probably the most significant indication of whether a behaviour management policy will make students feel they have a place and a voice or whether they will be further alienated. We need to look at whether the school is pastoral, punitive, points-driven or chaotic. In terms of discipline three elements that make up the climate of the school are of key importance. They are:

> leadership,
> the teaching and learning that goes on,
> the relationships that exist.

School Leadership

> There comes a time when 'firmness' may be appropriate, but a more fundamental task of the leadership is a clarification and a communication of the values and attitudes which are at the core of the school's policy on student behaviour and discipline. This process will be but a simple exercise for the school which has an up-to-date and 'owned' vision or mission statement.
>
> *Kavanagh (1993, p.66)*

The role of the school leader and the way in which he or she leads is also a significant factor in the success or failure of a discipline policy to have positive outcomes. Students learn very quickly whether or not the Principal is aware of what is going on around the school. As with the staff, students want a leader who knows them, is interested in their progress and makes them feel valued. The role taken up by management in ensuring that the discipline policy is carried out fairly and consistently is also of the utmost importance. Munn *et al.* (1992) point to the ways in which a school leader can influence behaviour for the better. They suggest the following:

- learning the names of all pupils

- being visible around the school

- using familiar language so that students do not feel alienated

- experimenting with and changing the curriculum

- offering a wide variety of extra-curricular activities

The school leader must also ensure that the potential for misbehaviour brought about by school-related factors is minimised. Teachers recognise that certain classes misbehave more in the afternoons than mornings; when they have had a "free" class; when the classroom is too hot, etc. It is the responsibility of the staff as a whole, but particularly the management, to minimise the impact of such factors.

Classroom Management

Teachers will find it most helpful to develop a classroom management plan. This could include seating arrangements for specific groups etc. They need to keep accurate records of any student misbehaviour, including the strategies used to improve behaviour and any relevant parental contact and outcome of that contact.

Both theory and practitioners emphasise the importance of classroom management. Those key people to whom the researcher spoke stressed the following points:

1. the importance of starting the lesson on time

2. the provision of appropriate seating arrangements

3. establishment of clear rules and procedures

4. a limit on the number of rules

5. teach the rules like academic content

If a mantra for the classroom practitioner were to be drawn up it might be as suggested below:

> **Get them in, get on with them, get on with it, get them out!**

The role of the teacher

> ...the teachers needed should be proud of the children they teach, pleased about becoming partners with their parents, and familiar with the neighbourhood in which they work. Further, teachers need to be active students of the resources in their school-communities, learn as much as they can about what their children are learning outside of school, and know how and under what conditions this learning takes place.
>
> *Haberman (1991, p.38)*

Second level teachers are faced with classrooms of teenagers with whom they have little in common. Even at primary level the apparent lack of respect for authority is evident. Understanding misbehaviour in the context of a child's life can lead to solutions in eliminating misbehaviour. In organisational terms the teacher can do a lot to minimise indiscipline. If there is a clear beginning to a lesson, a speedy start to get all students engaged in the task, there will be less opportunity for disruption. Experience and evidence show that the teacher who is adequately prepared, having chosen, to the best of his or her ability, material that is appropriate for the entire class group.

The teacher can also do much to defuse potential misbehaviour or conflict situations by adopting very low-key discipline techniques – the "look", a series of reminders, or perhaps ignoring, where to draw attention to a misdemeanour would be more disruptive to a classroom. The issue of "ignoring" misbehaviour is a difficult one. To ignore a once-off infraction, e.g. a curse not directed at anyone in the classroom, is not the same as ignoring small misbehaviours of children who are acting out to get attention. They will continue to misbehave until they gain the teacher's attention, with the misbehaviours becoming increasingly serious. We have to be conscious that "conflict in the classroom does not arise in a vacuum; it develops in a context. A serious breach of discipline is usually preceded by a series of small but significant incidents, in which students test the ground to see what the teacher is like and how much they can get away with". (O'Flynn and Kennedy, 2000, p.42)

Therefore, the role of the teacher in practical terms is essential. Far more important, however, is the relationship that the teacher builds with class groups and individuals. If we are seeking to engender a spirit of co-operation, self-discipline and community spirit in our students, they must first see it in us, their teachers.

Building Relationships

> The network of relationships and expectations amongst and between pupils, staff, parents and outside professionals, and the overall quality of pastoral care policies, are as influential in determining this climate as the impact of the formal curriculum and teaching skills of those who administer it.
>
> *Charlton and David (1993, p.233)*

The relationships which students enjoy with their teachers are the most significant relation-ships in the school organisation, at least where behaviour is concerned. For many students who experience home difficulties and poor standards of parenting, a smile or comment of approval may be the only positive connection with an adult which the student experiences all day. Therefore, the way in which teachers model behaviour towards others, especially the students in their care, is possibly the key factor in creating a climate where discipline can take place in a positive manner. In such an organisation punishment is used to deal with the act of misbehaviour in an appropriate way rather than the student in an inappropriate one.

Students constantly refer to problems with teachers being a significant issue in their misbehaviour. Certainly the attitudes and actions of some teachers do little to mirror the sort of behaviour we desire of our students. Too often the person at the head of the classroom uses sarcasm, ridicule and outright bullying to keep some form of order. "Once the notion of a teacher lacking respect for a pupil takes hold, it requires a lot of working through to overcome". (Klein, p.148) Charlton and David (1993, pp.232-233) emphasise the importance of relationships between everyone and at every level of the school community. Their recommendations for how teachers might better create positive relationships with their students might be a very good creed for all in the profession (Table 3).

Table 3	
Take the initiative:	**Do all you can to avoid:**
• greet and be greeted	• humiliating …it breeds resentment
• speak and be spoken to	• shouting …it can be counter-productive
• smile and relate	• over-reacting …the problems will grow
• communicate	• blanket punishments …the innocent will resent them
• use humour …it builds bridges	• sarcasm …it damages you.
• keep calm …it reduces tension	
• listen …it earns respect.	

Information Sheet

The following diagram outlines how the individual teacher's attitude and responses can impact on the way students behave.

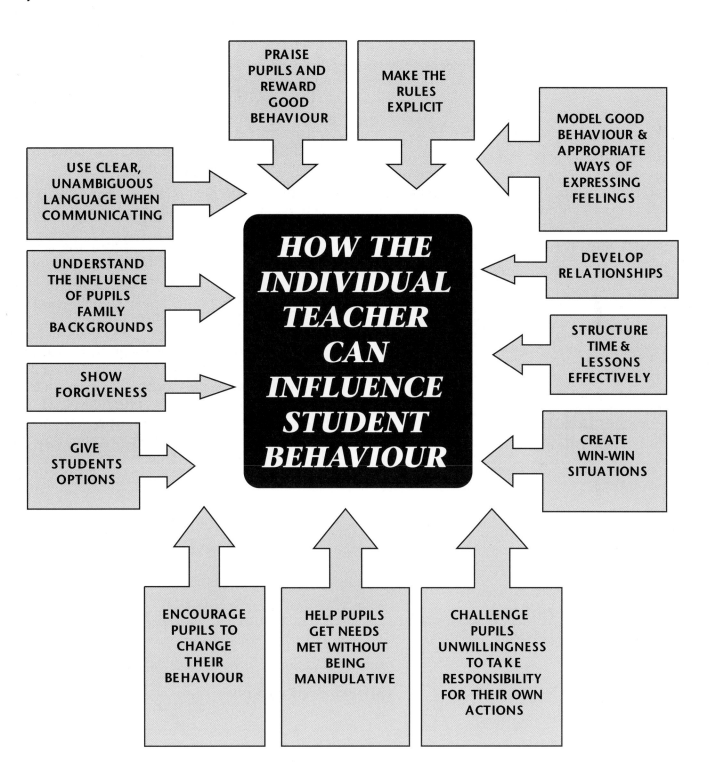

Information Sheet

The level of care present throughout the school organisation and the manner in which we deal with students and their behaviour as a whole community can also have a huge impact on whether even the mention of the word behaviour has positive or negative connotations.

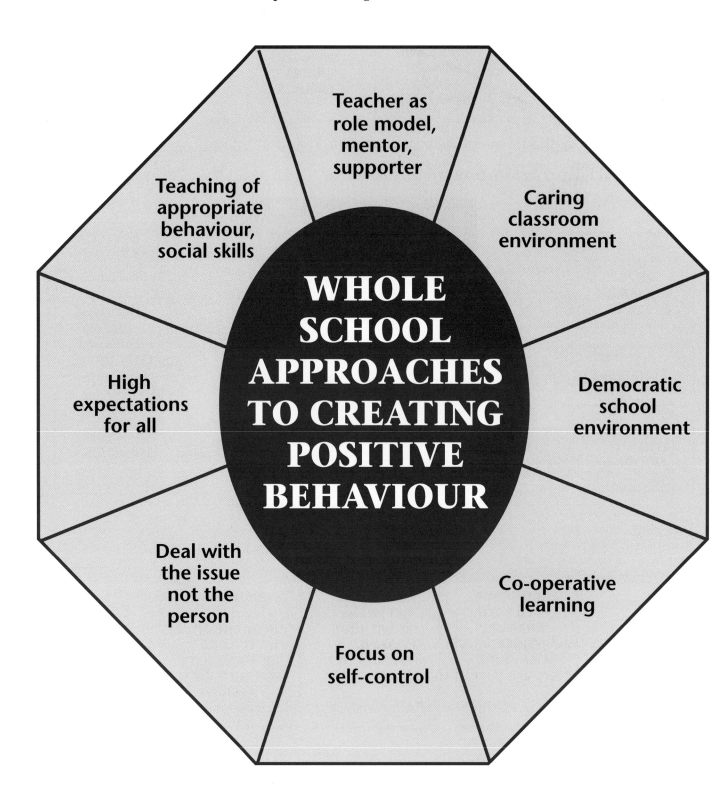

Information Sheet

DEVELOPING GOOD CLASSROOM MANAGEMENT STYLE
– THE LINK BETWEEN CURRICULUM & BEHAVIOUR

- Make sure you are not rewarding poor behaviour that is aimed at getting attention.

- Use a 'game' approach to get work completed where possible, e.g. word puzzles, wall charts etc.

- Change activities frequently so that boredom does not set in.

- Help with work before frustration sets in.

- Support a student who is having difficulty with encouragement.

- Set realistic goals so that success is guaranteed for all.

- Have three levels of achievement:
  - must know
  - should know
  - could know

- Allow an activity that students enjoy if other work is finished satisfactorily and on time.

- Don't lose your sense of humour and don't lose your temper. It doesn't work!

KEY QUESTIONS FOR TEACHERS

- ❑ What does the student need to learn?

- ❑ Where is the student now in relation to that target?

- ❑ What teaching approaches will you use?

- ❑ What factors are part of the plan?
  - strengths, personality, self-concept, physical needs, peers, parents, other people, etc.

- ❑ Does your goal make sense to the student?

- ❑ How will you ensure the student experiences success?

- ❑ How will you know the student is making progress?

Information Sheet

THE NEED TO HAVE HIGH HOPES - IS YOUR CLASSROOM MANAGEMENT STYLE DEVIANCE INSULATIVE?

Teachers and schools who model deviance-insulative behaviour

Allow face-saving
Avoid confrontations
Avoid differential treatment
Are optimistic
Believe that students really want to work
Encourage any sign of progress
Enjoy informal relationships, based on respect & humour
Minimum institutional control
Hesitation in enforcing rules likely to cause rebellion
Participation by both pupils and parents
High expectations of pupils' ability
Harmonious classroom where teachers are:
Composed
Impassive
Dispassionate
Serene
Unruffled
Shatterproof
Many tunes are possible

Adapted from Hargreaves

KEY QUESTIONS FOR TEACHERS

❏ **What does the student need to learn?**

❏ **Do I treat students fairly?**

❏ **Do I punish the whole class for the actions of an individual or a few?**

❏ **Do I focus on positive reinforcement of those who do behave?**

❏ **Is my classroom friendly but work oriented?**

❏ **Do I have high but realistic standards for all students?**

❏ **Do the students understand the routines I use in the classroom, e.g. collecting homework, writing homework into journal etc.**

❏ **Do I spend time teaching students the expectations I have around work and behaviour?**

❏ **Do I remind them of those expectations from time to time?**

Information Sheet

CONSIDER THE UNIQUE CHARACTERISTICS OF THE STUDENT

> **Strengths, skills, interests & weaknesses**
>
> **Physical, physiological, pharmacological make-up**
>
> **Verbal & other communication skills**
>
> **Social & self-management skills**
>
> **Support network**

- Does the difficult student have effective means of communicating with others? Does the student know what's expected? E.g. we may demand an apology; the student may not know how to do it.

- Does the student have a predictable daily routine?

- Does the student have experience with making choices in his/her life?

- Does the student have supports within the school? (peers, an adult)

- Does the student have regular opportunities for positive feedback and reinforcement?

- Does the student have basic survival social skills?
  - problem solving skills
  - anger management
  - relaxation techniques
  - self-control

- Does the student have a significant academic deficit?

- Need to look at how the student perceives his/her experience of school:
  - does he have favourite activities, subjects etc.
  - are there people in the school community with whom the student has a positive relationship?
  - what are the school settings which the student dislikes? E.g. large group, traditional didactic teaching methods etc.

- Employ strategies with the student, which are appropriate for the context - local norms, etc.

- Consider the goals and aspirations of the student, they may offer an opening into improved behaviour through motivation.

- Focus on the overall improvement of the student's lifestyle, options and choices

Information Sheet

STUDENTS' DESCRIPTION OF THEIR 'IDEAL' TEACHERS

The comments outlined below represent a cross-section of the views of students in some of the schools visited during the research phase.

- Caring – cares about you and your work

- Strict – they like you but they do not let you do what you like

- Well-organised – the lessons have a point to them

- Understanding/Good Listener/Fair

- Know how to apologise – admit it when they make mistakes

- Encouraging – say things like "We all make mistakes sometimes.

- Fun/Sense of humour – their lessons are interesting

- Respect – treat you like a person/don't put you down

- Have high standards – even if you're 'thick' they make you do your best/don't give you loads of copying just because you're in the bottom class

- Inspiring – makes you want to learn

- Treats the class with respect and respects you for what you are

- Tries to see pupils' point of view before giving up on them

KEY QUESTIONS FOR TEACHERS

Refer to the list of student descriptions of a 'good' teacher.

How do your actions in the classroom fit in with the profile?

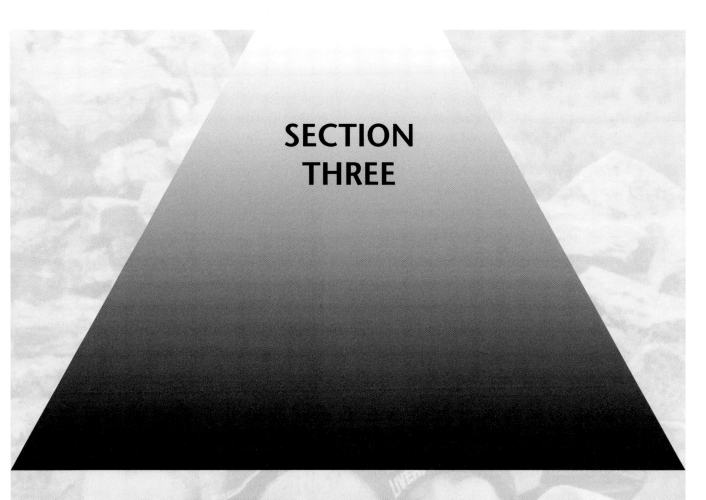

SECTION THREE

GLOBAL RESPONSES

Behaviour Management Systems around the world

Introduction

This section focuses on suggested responses to behaviour management in the form of approaches and systems used around the world. The material provides a starting point and topic for discussion at individual teacher and whole school level. It is intended that the descriptions would feed into any process.

Most teachers spend their time attending to pupils when they are not working or when they are being disruptive. Strategies which focus upon the positive and promote self-esteem are usually more successful than those which stress negative factors. There are a variety of behaviour management systems on offer, many of them with a positive emphasis at their core. It is worth looking at the key points of several, not only because they might provide a possible approach that an individual school might adopt, but also because they provide stimulus for discussion on the issue of behaviour and on how we approach relationships with young people. Various writers have advocated specific strategies of classroom management often based on experimental work and research. Some are of particular value in dealing with pupils with emotional and behavioural problems, learning disabilities or other special needs. There are many modifications of each and schools often adopt elements of one or more of the systems to suit their particular context.

Often these ideas are not new. Frequently when audits of behaviour are carried out it may become apparent that effective teachers, those who create positive atmospheres in their classrooms and who manage behaviour in a caring and decent way are using methods that are lauded by such systems. What is crucial is that such models are adapted to suit the context of the school and its stakeholders. None of these policies imposed from above on a school could have anything but the most superficial impact if the process of involving all members.

A summary of some of the more popular strategies is presented. Detailed explanations on a number of the programmes, e.g. The Good Behaviour Game and Token Economy are widely available on the internet. Other systems, notably Assertive Discipline, Discipline for Learning and Circle Time are available commercially, with a range of products and videos for sale from the originators.

Assertive Discipline

This American system is based upon the work of psychologist Lee Canter who has researched the characteristics of effective and successful teachers. Canter and his associates have prepared materials relating to classroom discipline and have conducted training sessions for teachers and other educators. In his book *Assertive Discipline: Positive Behaviour Management for Today's Schools* Canter claims that the most effective teachers are those who:

(a) set clear limits for behaviour at the very beginning of the year, i.e. they establish:

    (i) a list of about **five** cardinal rules (e.g. following instructions the first time they are given; keeping noise levels low; treating others with respect);

    (ii) an increasing scale of **five** penalties if children **choose** (with emphasis on the choice element) to break these rules, e.g. on the first breach of the rules the student receives a warning with his/her name written on a list or on the board. The second breach of the rules means 5 minutes detention during break time. The third breach of rules means isolation in a 'time-out behaviour modification unit' under the supervision of a senior member of staff. The fourth breach of the rules involves an interview with the principal. At the last breach of the rules parents are involved.

(b) enforce these rules, fairly and consistently;

(c) reinforce compliance with the rules and the completion of good work with praise. With younger pupils stickers, badges and good conduct points are used and with older children praise in assemblies, visits to the principal for praise and letters to parents.

(d) counsel pupils who are identified as having behavioural problems on a one-to-one basis. The aim is to help the pupil gain insight into the problem and to choose more responsible behaviour. Where appropriate, an individual behaviour plan is drawn up and parents are involved in supporting the programme.

Discipline For Learning

Developed by Adrian Smith of Teaching and Learning Associates, this model of behaviour management is popular with Irish schools. DFL seems more appropriate to primary, although there are examples of its use in the Irish secondary school setting, most notably the Greendale project. The system has the following core elements:

- Identify behaviour that is wanted
- Recognise behaviour that is not wanted
- An effective pastoral care system
- Use of whole school rewards
- Encourage all members of the school community to take responsibility for behaviour
- Emphasise consistency between home and school
- A focus on four pillars of good behaviour – good class work, behaviour, homework, attendance

(a) Rewards are given for good work and behaviour, e.g. brightly coloured stamps. Pupils receiving 50 stamps have their names entered for a draw for special prizes ranging from gift vouchers to an outing.

(b) Sanctions are known as consequences and escalate as follows:

   (i) A warning is given.

   (ii) A further violation of rules carries a 10-minute detention at the first available break time.

   (iii) A third breach of rules means a one-hour detention after school with 24 hours' notice to parents.

   (iv) A fourth consequence results in a further hour's detention and a letter home to the parents.

   (v) A fifth consequence carries a punishment of two or three days in isolation in a time-out unit.

Promoting Positive Behaviour In Schools

This scheme has been used since the late 1990s in secondary schools in Wales. The principal aims are to:

(a) develop a policy of rewarding good behaviour and imposing sanctions for anti-social behaviour. This policy is communicated to pupils and parents.

(b) identify pupils with problems at a very early stage.

(c) introduce social skills and personal problem solving to the curriculum

(d) make exclusion a last resort by involving the pupils and their parents

(e) a multi-agency approach to finding solutions to problems at home and in school.

Circle Time

Developed by Jenny Mosley & Barbara Maines among others, this model is popular in Irish schools and its use appears to be on the increase, both at primary and second level. It has 4 main aims:

- To build self-esteem
- To build self and group responsibility
- To promote good manners
- To encourage & emphasise creative talents

The lesson plans address themes such as:

- Friendship
- Bullying
- Homework
- Group rules
- Listening skills

CMCD – Consistency Management and Co-operative Discipline

Developed by Jerome Freiberg. Freiberg's belief is that we need to merge classroom, school, home and the community to support learners.

This model's primary objectives are:

- the prevention of misbehaviour
- the creation of a caring, co-operative community
- huge emphasis on prevention rather than intervention,
- shared responsibility,
- values-based discipline
- increased positive communication with parents.

Positive Discipline Programme

This programme, developed by Bill Rogers, aims to reduce the number of unnecessary emotional exchanges between students and teachers. Rogers asserts that the more teachers work at building relationships, the easier it is to teach and to control the classroom. If the teacher uses humour and is fair pupils will accept correction and consequences more positively since there is mutual respect.

Preventative Approaches to Disruption (PAD)

The PAD project by Barry Chisholm *et al.* is based upon certain of the ideas of John Robertson of Homerton College, Cambridge, and Professor Ted Wragg of the University of Exeter. The basic assumptions are that:

(a) **Prevention is better than cure**, i.e. it is better to identify and prevent disruptive behaviour from occurring than to have to deal with it once a situation has become serious.

(b) **Observation of good practice can be beneficial**, i.e. it is possible to look at teachers who are well organised and seem to have few problems of management and to describe what they are doing. It is then possible to list helpful codes of practice with respect to:

- verbal and non-verbal communication;
- lesson organisation;
- pupil management.

These three aspects of teaching all have importance for 'nipping trouble in the bud'.

PATHS – Promoting Alternative Thinking Strategies

This programme is designed to promote emotional & social competence and to reduce aggression & behaviour problems among primary school children. It is designed for children entering school and was developed by Mark Greenberg & Carol Kusché at the Center for the Study of Prevention of Violence, University of Colorado. Findings in the US have indicated that PATHS is effective both as a prevention and intervention programme.

The units cover 5 main areas:

- Self-control
- Emotional understanding
- Positive self-esteem
- Relationships
- Inter-personal & problem-solving skills

CBG ('Catch Them Being Good')

Diane Montgomery writes: "A child with high self-esteem is likely to be confident in social situations and enthusiastic in tackling new challenges in schoolwork. On the other hand, a child with low self-esteem will lack confidence in his or her ability to succeed, and as a result may try to avoid situations which present the possibility of failure". She advocates the system of CBG which requires teachers to take the following steps:

(a) **to reinforce positively a pupil's correct response**, e.g. smiles, nods, paraphrasing the pupil's answer and making affirming statements such as "Good", "Well done!". Teachers, she argues, should not dismiss or ridicule incorrect responses but encourage the pupil to try again with comments such as "Nearly" or "Good so far. Who can help him out?"

(b) **to move around the class**, to give encouragement by looking at the work of all pupils, not just those having difficulty or demanding attention. During the lesson the teacher should make personal, positive contact with every pupil by saying something supportive about their work and by listening to and receiving some of their thoughts about the activity.

(c) **to prevent the creation of a division between teacher and pupils.** While the class is working, the teacher does not stand or sit apart, but moves round the class, i.e. he/she moves into the class's territory. This avoids giving the message that "He/she is making us do this, but is not really interested as long as we finish it before the bell goes and keep quiet".

Montgomery also suggests that the teacher keep a tally of his/her positive comments by marking a sheet of paper with tally strikes or dots. Where the strategy is used successfully, it is argued that the use of CBG will outweigh any negative or 'desist' commands.

PCI (Positive Cognitive Intervention)

This strategy focuses upon the processes of learning (i.e. the way in which children learn something) as well as the product of the learning (i.e. the subject content). It is argued that much work in schools involves the learning of factual information, but pupils do not always see the point or relevance of what they learn. In such contexts they are less likely to co-operate with the teacher and discipline problems will arise. Indeed, it has been claimed that a high proportion of discipline problems can be related to pupils' inability to see the relevance of the activity set by the teacher.

It is therefore important to help pupils:

(a) realise the relevance of the work set (e.g. to everyday life, future careers, examination syllabuses);

(b) understand that their own efforts are an important and useful contribution to the successful completion of the activity.

Behaviour Modification

This approach to classroom management is derived from the research of psychologists such as B.E Skinner of Harvard University in the 1950s and 1960s. Desirable behaviour is rewarded and thus encouraged. Undesirable behaviour is disregarded. Behaviour modification has been used often in cases of children with emotional and behavioural difficulties [EBD] (e.g. aggressive behaviour). Basic steps in behaviour modification procedures are:

(i) the precise pinpointing by the teacher of behaviours which are desired (e.g. not speaking while the teacher is speaking) and those which are not desired (e.g. wasting time instead of completing work);

(ii) the making of an objective record of the frequency of these behaviours, e.g. by construction of a tally sheet. This permits the construction of baseline data which can be used to evaluate the effect of any behaviour modification programme;

(iii) the implementation of a specific programme of behaviour modification which will involve systematic reinforcement of the wanted behaviours (e.g. by providing rewards), thus practising the theory of operant conditioning that an individual will repeat acts which he/she finds personally rewarding;

(iv) the discontinuance of this programme, so that the teacher responds to the child in the usual way, as during the baseline. He/she again keeps a tally of the pupil's behaviour to evaluate the success of the behaviour modification at stage (iii);

(v) where the tally chart demonstrates that the behaviour modification programme works for the child, then the programme can be systematically resumed to improve behaviour further.

Behaviour modification techniques include:

(a) **The Rules + Ignore + Praise Approach:** Three main phases are utilised in this approach:

(i) Teachers specify rules so that pupils are fully aware of their expectations. Rules should be short, limited to about half a dozen and positively phrased (e.g. "Sit quietly while working").

(ii) Teachers ignore unwanted behaviour, unless there was the danger of injury to anyone in the room.

(iii) Appropriate behaviour is praised and the reason for the praise explained ("I like the way you're doing your work quietly John").

(b) **The Token Economy Approach:** In this approach the 'token' is anything such as a coloured disc which the pupil can exchange for some reward in order to reinforce good behaviour. When the pupil behaves as the teacher wants, he/she is rewarded with a token; if he/she behaves in an unacceptable manner, the token is taken away ('cost contingency').

This strategy has been used with children who appear to lack any basic interest in schoolwork. It has been used successfully with emotionally disturbed children to encourage them to respond to social rules.

(c) **The Contract System:** This involves an agreement between the child and the teacher that certain ways of behaving will result in certain consequences. The pupil is involved in negotiating the terms of the contract with the teacher.

This has been helpful in dealing with children from families where they do not learn to expect certain consequences as a result of certain actions or where control is arbitrary, leaving the child with no clear standards of behaviour.

Good behaviour is rewarded with praise at school assemblies and tangible rewards at the end of each term. In introducing the scheme the full co-operation of parents is essential.

(d) **The Good Behaviour Game** was developed by Barrish *et al*. Its aim is to reduce specific misbehaviour, e.g. undesirable noise and movement. This is done by:

(i) specifying rules of behaviour which are displayed around the room and to which reference is frequently made, e.g.

"We stay in our seats while working.

"We get on quietly with our work."

"We try not to interrupt."

(ii) setting a cassette tape which gives out a signal at irregular intervals, e.g. Whenever signal is heard, pupils at target tables who have adhered to the rules are awarded points by the teacher.

(e) **Pupil Self-Recording:** In this system the same methodology is used as in the good behaviour game, but the pupil involved is encouraged to record on a chart whether he/she was working when the signal was heard, i.e. an attempt is made to teach the pupil to self-record and monitor his/her own behaviour. This system requires the co-operation of the pupil, and, where it has been used successfully, teachers have initially pointed out to pupils the consequences of their undesirable behaviour and asked them if they want to change it. Where pupils co-operate, it has been an effective technique of behaviour modification.

These models are a good place for any staff to begin to form their own views of discipline in the classroom. Each teacher, each class, each subject, each situation is different but each model might have elements that may prove useful and appropriate now or in the future

A summary of the key ideas of several models of behaviour management which may prove useful in considering a school-specific model is included in the information sheets at the end of this section.

formation Sheet

ROGRAMME & UTHOR	UNDERLYING BELIEFS	OUTCOMES FOR STUDENTS
ssertive Discipline e & Marlene anter	Teachers should insist on responsible behaviour. Teacher is assertive rather than hostile or passive. State rules & expectations clearly. Apply positive consequences when expectations are met and negative consequences when they are not	Students should have advance knowledge of the consequences that will follow misbehaviour. Teachers will help students to limit inappropriate behaviour.
ircle Time eveloped by nny Mosley nong others	This model is popular in Irish schools. Lesson plans address themes such as: Friendship, Bullying, Homework, Group rules, Listening skills, Concentration	It has 4 main aims: Building self-esteem; Building self and group responsibility; Promoting good manners; Encouraging & emphasising creative talents
ooperative iscipline nda Albert ased on Adler, reikurs, Glasser tc.	Students must be affirmed & given opportunity to share responsibility for their own behaviour. Identify the goals of misbehaviour. Build student self-esteem. Involve teachers, students & parents in the process.	To belong. To feel capable of completing schoolwork. To feel that they connect with classmates and teachers. To know that they contribute to the group.
iscipline for earning eveloped by drian Smith of eaching and earning Associates	This model of behaviour management is popular with Irish schools. Identify behaviour that is wanted & recognise behaviour that is not wanted. A focus on four pillars of good behaviour – good class work, behaviour, homework, attendance	All members of the school community are encouraged to take responsibility for behaviour Emphasises consistency between home and school Have an effective pastoral care system
iscipline with ignity Mendler & Curwin ased on Glasser	All students must be treated with dignity regardless of their behaviour. Student involvement in the process; problem solving	To feel they are capable & successful; to know they are cared about by others; to realise that they are able to influence people & events
ids are worth it! arbara Coloroso	Students can develop self-discipline when treated with respect and given responsibility and choices. Showing students what they have done wrong. Show them how to solve problems. Leave their dignity intact.	Students need to hear the following messages: I believe in you. I trust in you. You are listened to. You are cared for. You are important.
ositive lassroom iscipline red Jones	Classroom management should be positive & gentle. Need to set limits. Need to build co-operation. Absence of coercion. Use of classroom structure. Setting limits. Incentives. Training students to take responsibility	Students will learn self-discipline within context of clear expectations. Students need consistent limits. Need to belong to a peer group, to co-operate with peers and make a positive contribution to the group.
eality Therapy x Discipline ill Glasser/ Robert Vubbolding	Genuine discipline is comes from making choices without infringing on the rights of others. Helps students to define their wants & needs, recognise their behaviours and plan to fix any problems.	To belong and to be involved with people. To achieve. To have fun.

OU MAY PHOTOCOPY THIS PAGE

Information Sheet

The Kounin Model: Withitness, Alerting and Group Management
♦ When you correct one pupil's behaviour, it tends to change the behaviour of others.
♦ The teacher needs to be *with it* to know what is going on everywhere in the room at all times.
♦ *Smooth transitions* between activities and maintaining momentum are key to effective group management.
♦ The most successful learning takes place when teachers keep pupils alert and held accountable for learning.
♦ There is a need for *variety* in lessons, the classroom environment and for pupils to be *aware of progress* they are making.
The Neo-Skinnerian Model: Shaping Desired Behaviour.
A recently popular outgrowth of Skinnerian behaviourism is Behaviour Modification.
♦ Behaviour is conditioned by its consequences. Behaviour is strengthened if followed immediately by reinforcement. Behaviour is weakened if it is not reinforced. Behaviour is also weakened if it is followed by punishment.
♦ In the beginning stages of learning, reinforcement provided every time the behaviour occurs produces the best results.
♦ Reinforcers include verbal approval, smiles, "thumbs up," prizes and awards.
The Ginott Model: Using Sane Messages
♦ Discipline is little-by-little, step-by-step. The teacher's self-discipline is key. Model the behaviour you want in students.
♦ Use *sane messages* when correcting misbehaviour. Address what the student is doing; don't attack the student's character [personal traits].
♦ Use communication that is *congruent* with student's own feelings about the situation and themselves.
♦ Invite co-operation rather than demanding it.
♦ Teachers should express their feelings—anger—but in sane ways. "What you are doing makes me very angry. I need you to...."
♦ Avoid sarcasm.
♦ Praise can be dangerous; praise the act, not the student and in a situation that will not turn peers against the pupil.
♦ Apologies are meaningless unless it is clear that the person intends to improve.
♦ Teachers are at their best when they help pupils develop their *self-esteem* and to trust their own experience.

The Glasser Model: Good Behaviour comes from Good Choices.

William Glasser's approach is worth serious consideration. It focuses on using class time to come up with a code of behaviour and a set of consequences to match. The thinking behind this model is being used successfully in a number of the schools visited.

- ♦ Students are rational beings capable of controlling their own behaviour.

- ♦ Help pupils learn to make good choices, since good choices produce good behaviour.

- ♦ Do not accept excuses for bad behaviour. Ask, "What choices did you have? Why did you make that choice? Did you like the result? What have you learned?"

- ♦ Reasonable consequences should always follow good or bad student behaviour.

- ♦ Class rules are essential to a good learning climate, they must be enforced.

- ♦ Classroom meetings are a good way to develop and maintain class behaviour.

Glasser's model encompasses 5 key questions which can prove useful starting points in any discussion of behaviour with pupils.

- ♦ What are you doing?

- ♦ What rule have you broken?

- ♦ What should you be doing?

- ♦ What can you do to fix the problem?

- ♦ What would you do differently next time?

Added to this Dreikurs, and later Albert, throw another question into the mix:

What can the teacher do to help you stay out of trouble and to help you succeed in class?

The Dreikurs Model: Confronting Mistaken Goals

- ♦ Discipline is not punishment. It means self-control.

- ♦ The teacher's role is helping pupils to impose limits on themselves.

- ♦ Teachers can model democratic behaviour by providing guidance and leadership and involving pupils in setting rules and consequences.

- ♦ All students want to belong. Their behaviour is directed to belonging.

- ♦ It is usually a mistake to assume that misbehaviour is an attack directed at the teacher. It is more likely to be an attempt at peer recognition.

- ♦ Misbehaviour is directed at mistaken goals: attention seeking, power seeking, revenge, and displaying inadequacy. The trick is to identify the goal and act in ways that do not reinforce mistaken goals.

- ♦ Teachers should encourage students' efforts, but avoid praising their work or character.

- ♦ Support the idea that negative consequences follow inappropriate behaviour by your actions.

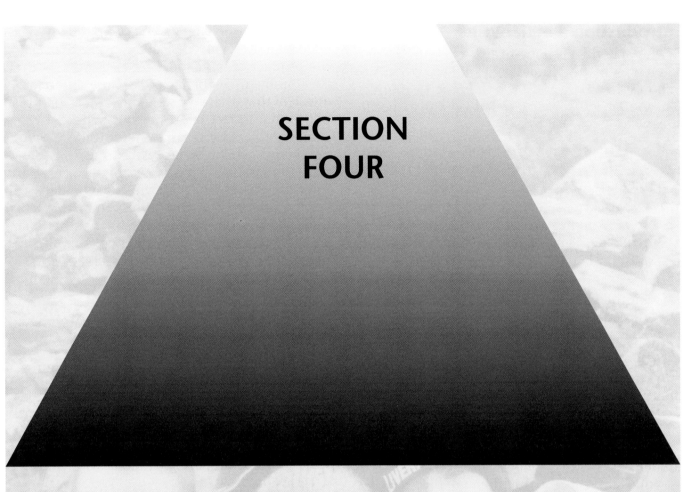

SECTION
FOUR

THE IRISH CONTEXT

Evidence of Best
Practice

Introduction – Initial Visits

The material outlined in the following section represents the findings of numerous visits to schools across Ireland over the past 15 months. The initial visits concentrated on three specific areas:

(i) the main concerns which those same schools had in terms of behaviour management

(ii) those current practices which schools felt were working well for them in terms of reducing misbehaviour and promoting positive behaviour

(iii) possible responses from the Christian Brothers Behaviour Management Project through the Centre for Education Services.

Although each of the schools operates in a different context and though they vary from primary to post-primary, urban to rural, north to south, there are clear similarities in terms of the key factors related to behaviour. The research uncovered many wonderful practices in terms of emphasising the positive and allowing every student to develop self-esteem and a sense of responsibility. It also highlighted the need for structures and consistency in managing behaviour. For example, from an organisational point of view the majority of secondary schools had a Year Head and Class Tutor/Class Teacher/Form Teacher system and there was a strong emphasis on helping those who are struggling either academically or in terms of behaviour, e.g. Learning Support, Counselling etc.

Other similarities are outlined below:

- the use of suspensions kept to a minimum
- clear guidelines established
- strong leadership
- extra-curricular activities
- mutual respect
- positive encouragement
- being prepared to listen
- an emphasis on pastoral care
- class teachers in an anchor role, positive rather than disciplinary
- the recognition that there is a need for rules
- the importance of homework
- high expectations of pupils

Many of the behaviour codes in schools with good practice evolved steadily rather than being the product of a one-off staff meeting to address the 'problem' of behaviour. Those interviewed attested that there was no neat start or finish point, that in fact the behaviour policy is always subject to review and modification where necessary – that the process is ongoing. Hence the emphasis on process in this project. Early indications are that if the stakeholders can become involved in the process the policy is far more likely to be implemented across the board and to become part of the school's day to day workings, consistently applied by all.

What was apparent from those schools where behaviour was managed in a positive way were those factors which were common to all, irrespective of context:

- emphasis on creating and maintaining a positive school ethos
- the teaching of correct behaviour, rather than punishing wrong behaviour
- the presence of a mechanism for student voices to be heard, e.g. Student Council, Circle Time etc.
- the use of the Homework diary/School Journal as an integral part of the behaviour policy and a key means of communicating with parents
- the existence of Class Tutor/Year Head systems and the use of a 'ladder of referral' so that the Principal dealt with only very serious incidents or persistent offenders who had been referred on
- wide variety of extra-curricular activities
- availability of other facilities, e.g. Breakfast Club, After-school clubs, Homework clubs, often run by senior students who thrived on the responsibility and trust afforded them
- the supporting of innovative ways to create better relationships, e.g. student councils, circle time etc.
- a clear set of school strategies for dealing with the 5% or so of pupils who cannot flourish even under positive behaviour systems
- the use of rewards and affirmation
- the emphasis on classroom management and student-teacher relationships as the key to better whole-school behaviour

Many of the schools, whether consciously or unconsciously, operated their behaviour management system on the belief that by praising and rewarding acceptable behaviours such behaviour can become the norm. One primary school's thinking around creating a positive atmosphere is outlined below:

- Don't wait for perfection – with a difficult pupil you might have to wait forever!
- Reward and recognise a variety of things, not just academic or sporting.
- Screen for skills, interests, and positions of responsibility outside school.
- Record any achievement – display photos, poems, drawings etc.
- Use a range of 'posts of responsibility' to show the child he/she is valued:
  - homework assistant – collects copies
  - register/roll book assistant
  - communications assistant – messages
  - equipment assistant – handing out & collecting materials
  - environment assistant – watering plants etc.

These jobs can be rotated so that every member of the class takes on some responsibility during each term.

The summary below highlights the type of practical activities and programmes those schools have undertaken in order to build relationships and community.

PRIMARY

- Awards schemes – some based on DFL – use of points, stickers, merits – prizes such as trips to cinema, adventure activities, pens, vouchers etc.
- Réalt na Seachtaine
- Boy of the Week/Student of the Month/Boy of the Year
- Good News postcards
- Certificates – Best Endeavour/Most Improved etc.
- Photographs of success displayed on walls
- Displays of pupils' work
- Rise 'n' Shine Club
- No Blame Bullying Policy
- Circle Time
- Choosing Time
- Art Therapy
- Music Therapy
- Drama classes / Drama productions 4 to 5 times a year – parents see the positive

- Creativity in the Classroom
- Use of yellow & red cards
- Conscious effort to have fewer suspensions – focus on the positive
- Care & Respect for all.

POST-PRIMARY

- Ladder of referral – subject teacher – Class Tutor – Year Head – Deputy Principal – Principal
- Pastoral Care & Discipline seen as equally important
- Weekly Year Head meetings & class tutor system – emphasis on creating a positive climate
- Role of class tutor expanded – more emphasis on pastoral – allocated time with class for SPHE, RSE & general building of relationships
- Emphasis on extra-curricular activities – a belief that they create good teacher-student relationships
- Sports clubs/Choir/Homework Club/After-school study/Breakfast club
- Involvement with outside agencies & projects – Trinity Access Programme/Business in the Community/Mentoring/Dublin Schools Business Partnership/Pathways through Education/
- Student ID cards to monitor attendance & punctuality
- Use of Homework Diary as point of contact with parents & record keeping
- Weekly newsletter item, focusing on what has improved & acting as a reminder of what to work on
- Award schemes, e.g. Homework Shield/Most Determined/'Picasso Award' for best artist of the year etc.
- Behaviour Slips – good as well as bad – forwarded to relevant Year Head
- Emphasis on why the rules are there – discussed with students
- Students given an opportunity to come up with alternatives
- The notion of 'community service' as a consequence
- Care Room
- Student Council involvement in devising policy

Of course, irrespective of the successes experienced by schools visited none had the solution to every behavioural difficulty. The main concerns which were repeated frequently centred on the impact of legislation on the school's code of behaviour, and the sense that a school's code now has to be a 'catch all', outlining every possible type of misbehaviour and appropriate sanction in order to satisfy that legislation. Concern was also expressed about the increasing number of students presenting with emotional and behavioural difficulties, and the problems encountered in getting appropriate psychological assessment and ongoing help for such students. Teachers felt that they were increasingly asked to adopt a multitude of roles in dealing with students particularly those who misbehave. Those roles included social worker, psychologist, parent, detective and judge. They felt ill equipped to take on such roles and so the need for training and development of coping mechanisms was another of the main concerns which are outlined below:

ISSUES OF CONCERN

- Implications of recent legislation such as Education Act, Education Welfare Act & Equality Act.
- Fear that legal requirements will make dealing with misbehaviour even more difficult
- The provision of sample policies
- The need for extra psychological assessment for students
- The need to create behavioural units for those pupils who cannot cope with school irrespective of efforts at positive behaviour
- The need for training and professional development for staff on behaviour issues

The third focus of the initial research was to ask Principals, teachers and students what they felt would be appropriate responses to the behavioural difficulties their schools and others were experiencing. Their viewpoints and suggestions have informed the work of the project since its inception and were also useful in designing the audit materials outlined in Section 6. A range of those suggestions is presented below:

Suggested Responses To The Problems Encountered In Managing Behaviour

- Letting people see what is best practice elsewhere
- Opportunity to gain a view of students' perceptions on behavioural issues.
- Staff training on issues related to behaviour
- Help with developing policy
- Help with producing Codes of Behaviour which are student & parent friendly
- Provision of Resources – worksheets, posters, ideas that are practical & could be adapted & used in any classroom.
- More development on pastoral care to alleviate the inequality & unevenness of roles, e.g. Class Tutor and Year Head
- Appropriate support for kids with 'coping' difficulties
- Reduced numbers of subjects for students who are not coping with academic life
- Reduced class sizes
- 'Chill Out' rooms in schools – computers, resources etc.
- Behavioural experts and resource teachers to move around schools, working with staff and students.
- Development of a highly stocked 'roving centre'
- 'Roving' subs who would be highly trained & would come into schools for a period of time to give teachers support
- An immersion programme for decision-makers & DES people to see what behaviour problems are really like.

A unique aspect of the Christian Brothers Behaviour Management Project is that it could respond to and deliver on some of the suggestions almost immediately. Some schools have already engaged in training on issues such as classroom management techniques, implications of legislation, the changing context of behaviour management etc. In other cases small groups of teachers have sought professional development on factors such as dealing with 'weaker' students and the role of multiple intelligences. Resources, a sample of which are included in Section 7, have been designed and made available to schools. Work has also taken place on the design and presentation of codes of behaviour. Other schools have undertaken the full process model outlined in this pack. The Centre of Education Services and the Education Offices of the Christian Brothers network are examining how some of the other responses outlined above might be delivered through the project in the future. **Among the services already available through the Centre for Education Services at Marino are:**

Facilitation:

school management team

year head team

class tutor team

pastoral care team

discipline committees

student councils

Boards of Management

Trustees

Staff Development:

conflict management

building collaboration

improving communication

stress management

Training:

classroom management

year head and tutor teams

pastoral teams

building relationships

Process Particular Issues:

school culture

team building

addressing conflict

Ethos and characteristic spirit

Information Sheet

CLEAR GUIDELINES COMING FROM RESEARCH

In 'best practice' schools there is a belief that good discipline is inherently linked to a good climate and positive relationships within the school community. Among the methods used to create such climates are:

- Daily routines, e.g. whole school assemblies, year assemblies, class group meetings, registration time used constructively etc.

- Recognition that students need to feel and be valued.

- High expectations of students in terms of behaviour & work rate.

- The recognition and praise of good behaviour.

- A need for consistency and clear limits.

- Appropriate sanctions, well understood by students, teachers and parents.

- Opportunities for students to assess their own behaviour and understand the consequences of their actions.

- Sanctions to be followed up with opportunities for students to work out more positive ways of behaving.

- Teachers as role models in terms of behaviour.

Information Sheet

Voices From The Chalk Face

SCHOOL EXPERIENCES OF DEVELOPING POLICY

- The need to market the policy internally – to the 'silent majority' of students who do behave

- The need to give priority to the prevention of problem behaviour

- The need to see how students perceive misbehaviour

- The need to ask students what expectations they have of each other – you may be surprised by their high standards

- The need to use discussion groups, tutor group meetings, questionnaires so that you can look at issues of injustice with students and look at strategies for specific areas, e.g. classroom, corridors, playground, cafeteria etc.

- The need for the merit/award system to be written into the behaviour system – making sure that the award system rewards behaviour and other aspects of school life, not just academics

- The need for very clear levels and ceilings at which each individual member of staff has authority & responsibility – those levels signalled very clearly to students

- 'it doesn't matter what the system is once it's apparent to everyone'

- 'if you're going to start new procedures in September you should start the planning and the process before christmas of the previous year'

- The need for 'consultation routes' to remain once the process is over and procedures are in place

SECTION
FIVE

FROM PROCESS TO POLICY

A Process Model

A Selection of Case Studies & Examples

Developing Policy – A step by step checklist

Introduction

Much of the research and fieldwork undertaken over the first fifteen months of the project highlighted the importance of a process model being used to arrive at a Code of Behaviour. Even where a specific system had been brought in from outside it had more often than not been adapted, reviewed and developed to suit the context of the school. This section outlines a model whereby all stakeholders in a school can become involved in the process of designing policy so that it can be implemented effectively and become truly embedded in the life of the school.

Legal Requirements

The issue of suspensions and expulsions will become increasingly important for schools in the future as legal requirements reduce the flexibility of Principals and Boards of Management. The Education (Welfare) Act, 2000 requires the Board of Management of every school to prepare a code of behaviour. That code of behaviour should be drawn up after consultation with the principal, teachers, parents and educational welfare officer and should specify:

- the standards of behaviour that shall be observed by each student attending the school

- the measures that may be taken when a student fails to observe those standards

- the procedures to be followed before a student may be suspended or expelled from the school concerned

- the grounds for removing a suspension imposed in relation to a student

- the procedures to be followed relating to notification of a child's absence from school.

Parents of prospective pupils should be provided with a copy of the code of behaviour, may be required to confirm in writing that the code is acceptable to them and shall make all reasonable efforts to ensure compliance with such code by the child.

The Department of Education of Northern Ireland highlights the need for Boards of Governors and Principals to take cognisance of both *The Health and Safety at Work (N.I.) Order 1978* and *The Education (N.I.) Order 1998, Article 3* in their dealings with behaviour. The statutory responsibilities include a common law duty of care towards pupils and a responsibility to ensure the safety of their teachers and other employees.

DENI outlines the need for each Northern Ireland school to produce a written statement on pupil behaviour and discipline, drawn up in consultation with parents. Such statements will allow schools to determine the measures they will take to:

- Promote pupil self-discipline & respect for authority

- Encourage good behaviour and respect for others

- Secure acceptable standards of behaviour among students

Many of the schools within the preliminary research group are making concerted efforts to reduce the number of suspensions and expulsions. This effort at reducing out-of-school consequences comes as a result of the increased legal pressures, but more importantly from the recognition by both Christian Brothers and other schools, that in-school consequences for misbehaviour can be more constructive and have more positive outcomes for students. There are also issues around what students who have been expelled or are suspended do while out of school. Schools are increasingly seeing suspension as a last resort and they take into account the fact that time out of school may be spent in less than useful pursuits. The issue of non-supervision is particularly relevant in the current economic climate given that many households have both parents working. Among the questions to be answered include:

- are students on suspension supervised at home?

- are they free to wander around unsupervised?

- are they in the company of young people who have already dropped out of school?

Given the impact of legislation several important tenets must apply in the development of a school-wide behaviour policy, its introduction and implementation.

- All stakeholders must have ownership of the policy, having been involved in its development and its implementation. There must be student and parent input.

- All members of the school staff must have access to professional development in effective classroom and behaviour management. This might include giving staff an opportunity to explore and understand personality types, teaching and learning styles, multiple intelligence theory etc.

- The code must be fair, with logical consequences for those who misbehave.
- The code should emphasise the positive, with appropriate recognition for the majority of pupils who behave.
- The policy must be widely disseminated among the staff, students, parents and any other stakeholders.
- Steps must be taken to ensure that the code is fairly and consistently enforced.

Collaboration With Other Stakeholders

Research and practice indicate that the early involvement of and consultation with parents in the behaviour planning process maximises the opportunities to modify students behaviour. Among the questions which staff, parents and pupils need to consider are the following:

- What are acceptable boundaries of good behaviour?
- Will there be systematic giving of rewards in order to modify behaviour?
- How does curriculum influence behaviour?
- In what ways does classroom management need to change?

- How does the school's ethos influence behaviour?
- How will links with home be used to enhance positive behaviour?
- How will pastoral care fit with a positive behaviour management programme?

They will have to come to agreement on

- a proactive approach rather than a reactive approach
- the school ethos or characteristic patterns of behaviour
- the planned routines and structures
- the spirit of the intervention rather than the letter
- the sharing of responsibility
- the use of rewards rather than sanctions
- the quality of teaching and learning
- the affective or pastoral dimension in the school
- pupil involvement in the life of the school
- parental involvement in the life of the school

The process model which has been piloted through the project follows and examples and case studies are offered to illustrate how process and policy work in tandem.

Developing A School Wide Behaviour Management System – Process For Policy

Formation of committee – Might include experienced teachers, new teachers, guidance staff, resource teachers etc – a mixture is ideal, each will bring a different perspective.

Review of the current provisions for behaviour management – what works well/what needs to be tightened up?

List of clearly defined priorities in terms of modifying/developing the Code of Behaviour

Working group to put together the views and suggestions of all involved in the school community – the involvement of parents and students is essential

Development of a behaviour code that helps students to understand the school's expectations and display desired behaviours – to include the logical consequences of misbehaviour & positive recognition for those who behave

Proposed code to be brought back to all stakeholders in draft form for further consultation and response – allows for re-engagement with the partners

Agreement of all partners to introduce the new whole school policy

Develop total staff commitment to the new approach

Engage in an awareness/training programme

Following the process there will be:

> **A written policy agreed upon by the school community**
>
> **A student handbook**
>
> **A staff handbook**
>
> **Forms to be used in the programme**

The creation of such handbooks and material should not impede the introduction of the policy. Very often schools get bogged down in the creation of the 'perfect' behaviour policy (if such a thing exists) to the detriment of its ever being implemented across the whole school. Fullan's notion of 'Ready, Fire, Aim' is one that might be applied in this case. To delay too long in the introduction of a policy may result in a loss of enthusiasm on behalf of staff members who are not involved in the writing up of ideas and policy but who are waiting to implement change.

Why Bother With Process?

- Working through a process rather than rushing to policy will allow for the design of a clear timetable for review, recommendations and implementation
- It will help the school understand what is working well already
- It will help the school to identify areas for improvement and development
- It will help the school adapt to the changing circumstances which all schools are experiencing
- It will allow the school community to set achievable and identifiable targets
- It will provide criteria for measuring the effectiveness of any changes, e.g. more displays of student success, fewer suspensions etc.
- A policy that is achieved through collaboration will clearly be more attractive to teachers, students and parents.

Case Study 1 – From Process to Policy

Riverview College is a community school in the tradition of Edmund Rice and Nano Nagle. It was established through an amalgamation in 1998 and has a current student intake of 720 students. A new Principal was appointed in 2000. The Code of Discipline established for the school at the time of amalgamation took what was perceived as best practice from both existing codes and attempted to marry them together. Recognising that the school has developed since the amalgamation and mindful of the changes in education and impact of legislation on schools it was decided to revise the Code of Discipline during the school year 2001-2002.

In November 2001 a facilitator from the Marino Institute Centre for Education Services visited the school to meet with Principal and Deputy-Principal as well as those staff members willing to be involved on the Behaviour Management working party. It had been suggested by the facilitator that the working party should represent all strands of staff member, from Assistant Principal to part-time teacher and there was one representative from each sector. The initial meetings were a chance for the facilitator to get a sense of management and staff concerns around the issue of behaviour and to work out a framework which would take the school through the process of examining current practices and developing policy for the future. A further meeting with the working party took place before a whole staff day was given over to the issue of behaviour.

The initial whole staff development day had as its objectives:

- To review current practices
- To explore possible rules, rewards and consequences in keeping with a positive focus on behaviour
- To outline a timetable for moving the process forward so that it would include parents and students.

The review of current practices highlighted several aspects of the existing system that were working well, e.g. the ladder of referral from

Subject Teacher to Tutor to Year Head and above. Other positives were the Principal's highlighting of student successes in many facets of school life at assemblies, over the intercom and in weekly news reports read at tutor time.

Staff felt that the use of the journal and record keeping could be tightened up. Significantly, staff recognised that there was scope to be more positive towards the majority of students in the school who did meet expectations in terms of behaviour. Concern for the 'middle muddlers', those students who often slip through the net was voiced. Staff acknowledged that there were too many rules and that the existing system was mainly sanction driven.

In terms of short term planning targets on record keeping and consistent use of the homework journals were set – to be reviewed at the next full staff meeting. It was decided that the working party, along with the facilitator, would draw up a questionnaire to seek the views of students and parents.

Staff members were also asked to reflect privately on their own classroom management styles and consider the type of climate which existed in their own classrooms.

A second whole staff meeting was convened one month later with the objective of reaching a consensus on a reduced, positively framed set of rules. Each staff member listed and ranked those misbehaviours which he/she found particularly disruptive. Group discussion followed around designing six essential rules. There was some difficulty in drawing up the list using positive language and several staff members felt that a list of 'Ten Commandments' or 'Seven Deadly Sins' would be more appropriate. Once six rules had been agreed, a comparative list of sanctions to deal with misbehaviour was drawn up. Both lists were to be circulated to other members of the school community.

The working party had designed questionnaires to be distributed to parents and students. The student questionnaire was administered on the same time afternoon to all students present. Parent questionnaires were sent home via students. When this method returned a low response rate it was decided to target parents attending a number of parent-teacher meetings over the coming fortnight. Parents could fill in the survey while waiting to see staff members. The Home School Liaison teacher was assigned to explain the purpose of the questionnaire and to collect them where possible. Two members of the Behaviour Working Group took responsibility for collating and analysing the parent question-naires, while the facilitator dealt with the student responses. Staff expressed surprise at the positive nature of the comments. A sample of responses to the request to describe a 'caring teacher' demonstrate how teacher and student percep-tions might not be so far apart.

> **Doesn't want you to get C's and D's on your report, and get grounded and not get any pocket money.**
>
> **Takes the time to talk to parents and tells them what the student needs to do to succeed.**
>
> **Doesn't shout when you are the only one who does not understand something. Instead takes you aside and helps you understand.**
>
> **If you are bad in school, calls your parents because they care about your behaviour.**
>
> **Says 'Good job!' when you do well.**
>
> **Will notice when something is wrong with you**
>
> **Is on your back a lot – tells you what to do, tells you to work harder.**

Class teachers used the weekly tutorial time to discuss the suggested rules and sanctions with class groups. Those sessions were also used to explore the possibility of introducing a rewards system and other methods of recognising student achievement. These issues were also discussed with the parents' council.

With all of the data gathered and discussions completed a pilot Code of Behaviour and rewards system was tested during the final term of 2001-2002. The policy was monitored during the trial period. Referrals to senior management were lower, as were the number of detentions and suspensions. Students and parents were happy that the new positive focus highlighted numerous student successes, not just the academic. A final whole staff meeting was held in May 2002 to evaluate the new code. Any necessary changes were made before it was adopted for the next school year. The final policy was then sent to the Board of Management for approval.

The effort put into involving all members of the school community in drawing up the code led to a genuine sense of ownership. The emphasis on positive expectations and student responsibility was welcomed by teachers and parents. A staff development day to explore further the notion of positive behaviour and creating positive relationships in school was held in September 2002, thus building on the work of the initial process. The rewards system has been expanded to allow for categories where students nominate peers.

Case Study 2 – the problem with policy before process, a rewarding outcome?

Rice Academy is an all-boys school in the midlands with a student population of just over 500. In September of 2001 a Rewards System was introduced by the newly appointed Principal. His rationale was clear. While discipline was a strong feature of the school and he wished it to remain so, the current system was very prescriptive and sanction laden. Over the course of that introductory year the Merits System which awarded students certificates based on the commendations of their teachers ran apparently successful. Students were awarded Commendations (10 merits); Bronze Certificate (25 merits); Silver Certificate (50 merits); Gold Certificate (75 merits) and Platinum Certificate (100 merits). Students were also awarded prizes such as pens, sweets and vouchers. Teachers and students participated readily in the scheme. At the end of the year the Principal decided to evaluate the impact of the programme on all students and examine their awareness of the scheme. A simple questionnaire was administered to all students.

- 24% of students did not understand the behaviour policy and rewards system.

- 27% of students had not had more than one merit over the entire course of the year. Most of those students were in the middle streams. Students who had already been identified as having behavioural difficulties had also failed to gain many rewards.

- 15% had been awarded a Bronze Certificate or higher. Most of this group consisted of the academic 'high flyers' and those students who were particularly weak, i.e. the 'special' class. It seemed the cumulative element of the system was too difficult for the majority of students.

- Few 5th or 6th Year students had been rewarded.

- Not surprisingly the rewards were most valued by 1st Years. By 3rd Year students did not highly value being rewarded through the system. It seems that since teachers knew the rewards were not valued by 5th & 6th Years they had abandoned it in practice.

- The perception of most students was that the rewards were for the academically able and those with sporting talents. They felt they had little chance of gaining rewards therefore there was no real motivation in the system.

Students were also asked to outline what they felt were effective rewards:

1st to 3rd Years	a positive letter home pens & stationery sweets extra computer time free time vouchers
5th & 6th Years	vouchers/money privileges letter home – often associated with financial reward activities/visits to cinema

The responses from the students, along with the realisation that many teachers were not applying the rewards system in the senior school, necessitated a complete overhaul of the whole behaviour management system. While it was recognised that praise and rewards had a place in the school it was recognised that for the outcome to be positive for all students it needed to be designed with all of them in mind. Over the course of the next academic year all members of the school community were engaged in looking at what was working well and what needed improvement in terms of the overall code of behaviour. Staff, students and parents also drew up a more meaningful rewards system which targeted many aspects of school life and student participation, not just sports or academics. The new rewards system included an element of peer commendation and recognition and has been successfully piloted among all students.

Case Study 3 – parental perceptions of communication with the school

St. Cornelius School was aware that the number of parents attending school activities, including parent-teacher meetings had been falling significantly over the past couple of years. Attempts to use different times and venues so as to cater for increasing numbers of working parents had not brought any significant results, nor had inviting parents to the school in small groups according to their child's class rather than to whole school meetings. With the help of the Home School Liaison teacher a sample of 100 parents (20 from each year group) was surveyed to examine communications between school and home, and to explore whether relationships between school and home were more positive than negative, or vice versa.

Of the 100 parents surveyed only 48% felt that communication between school and home was more positive than negative. In terms of breakdown of year groups figures were as follows:

	felt communication more positive than negative
1st year	65%
2nd year	56%
3rd year	42%
5th year	33%
6th year	45%

In terms of category of student/perception of student, figures were as follows:

Students with behavioural difficulties	5%
Students with recognised learning disabilities	70%
High achieving students	75%
Middle achieving students	23%
Low achieving students	65%

The low perception of positive communication from school of the parents of those students in the middle academic streams pointed to the danger that those 'middle muddlers' were getting lost. While high achievers and those with specific learning difficulties were well catered for there seemed to be evidence that those in the middle streams were in danger of being lost. Perhaps not surprisingly the parents of those students who had behavioural problems felt that communication from school had been almost entirely negative.

It was felt that action needed to be taken. Over the course of the following term various ideas were tried including a newsletter home emphasising positive activities of all years and ability levels; 'good news' postcards sent to all students regularly and a renewed attempt to organise a more representative Parents Committee.

An action plan to improve communications throughout the school community and between all of its members was put in place. Among the targets was the creation of a Parents' Room in the school to provide a non-threatening venue for meetings. A former classroom near reception has now been transformed into a bright, welcoming place, with the aid of some funding from the Stay in School Retention Initiative. Efforts to increase parental participation continue and attendance at the monthly Parents Committee meetings has increased fourfold, albeit from three to twelve! The struggle continues.

Information Sheet

Suggested Process for Development and Implementation of a Whole-School Behaviour Policy
A facilitator/key person offers to oversee the project
Key person works with an action group/working party
Working party reviews behaviour management in operation throughout the school: **in the classroom** **around the school** **with individual children**
Whole staff reviews current practices
Consultation with the whole-school community to determine priorities, map out the policy and draws up action plan and targets.
Policy is rewritten or drawn up, piloted, monitored, evaluated, adapted and adopted.

Information Sheet

THE PROCESS – STEP BY STEP REALITY

The process for the development of the plan often looks as follows:

Step 1 – A member of the Centre for Education Services at Marino Institute of Education is hired as the consultant. He/she carries out an audit of staff's perceived needs around behaviour management.
(N.B. In some cases an audit is also carried out with other members of the school community, in particular students & parents).

Step 2 – Members of staff are invited to volunteer to work with the consultant regarding the school-wide behaviour management plan.

Step 3 – Volunteers (hereafter known as "the discipline steering group") meet with the consultant at regular lunch meetings to provide recommendations and guidance regarding the proposed behaviour management plan.

Step 4 – Consultant assists the steering group to develop a working document for distribution to a range of stakeholders in the school community, including parents and students.

Step 5 – Stakeholders provide feedback to the "steering group" who direct the consultant as to how to rewrite the working document to reflect the input.

Step 6 – The revised behaviour plan document is submitted to all members of the school community (including parents council, student representatives, secretarial staff & all ancillary staff) and other interested parties for their comments.

Step 7 – The "steering group" works with the consultant to rewrite the working document to incorporate feedback from the school community.

Step 8 – Inservice training/staff development is undertaken. Handbooks and other materials are developed by committees.

Step 9 – The school-wide behaviour management plan is implemented.

Step 10 – The plan is frequently evaluated by committee and revised as necessary.

Information Sheet

Sample Staff Development Day

St. Edmund's Academy
Staff Day

9.30 am   Introduction

9.40 am   Behaviour Management in a Changing Context
– societal & legislative changes

11.00 am   Coffee

11.20 am   Reviewing Current Practices

1.00 pm   Lunch

2.00 pm   Developing our rules, sanctions and rewards

3.00 pm   Working towards whole school consensus

3.30 pm   The way forward: Conclusion & evaluation

nformation Sheet

SAMPLE ACTION PLAN

PRIORITY: TO IMPROVE BEHAVIOUR				
TARGET: TO IMPROVE ATTENDANCE BY 10%				
Tasks	**Who**	**When**	**Resources**	**Success Criteria**
1. Improve registration & record keeping ➦ Call roll before every class ➦ Send absentee list to office after every class ➦ Carry out spot checks	All staff Year Head with responsibility for attendance Deputy Principal	From January	Computer system Time – teachers & secretary	Attendance up to 90% All staff maintaining accurate records Attendance Reward Scheme in place
2. Improve communications with parents re attendance ➦ Produce standard letters re absence ➦ Request meeting with parents of chronic absentees ➦ Explain implications of Education Welfare Act to all parents via information sheet sent home	Principal, Deputy Principal, Year Heads & Tutors Home School Liaison Officer	During Spring term	Time – class tutors, Year Heads, secretary Stationery Postage	**Monitoring Procedures** Weekly review of attendance figures, monthly meeting to discuss chronic cases
3. Encourage improved attendance ➦ Introduce rewards system for good attendance	Tutors & Year Heads	From February Mid-Term Break	Certificates Vouchers Other prizes	**Evaluation** Numbers of absentees monitored to compare with old system

Adapted from the work of the School Development Planning Initiative

FROM PROCESS TO PRODUCT
WHAT A BEHAVIOUR POLICY SHOULD CONTAIN

A behaviour policy should contain the following elements:

- The general aims of the school
- A description of the rights and responsibilities of all members of the school community
- Rules or a code of conduct
- A description of the ways in which the school encourages good behaviour
- Rewards for good behaviour
- A description of unacceptable behaviours
- The consequences of misbehaviour
- Mechanisms for achieving a supportive culture and positive learning environment
- A description of the school's approach to positive behaviour management
- Strategies to respond to diversity and difference within the school community
- Strategies for the prevention of bullying and other serious misbehaviour
- Processes for resolving conflict
- Procedures for informing and involving parents
- Details of assistance available to staff, students and parents
- Mechanisms for monitoring and reviewing the behaviour management plan
- Links to other policies, e.g. Substance Misuse, Bullying etc.

The Issue of Rights & Responsibilities

These should be designed based upon the values and ethos of the school. They might include

- Mutual respect
- Respect for property
- Self-respect
- Fairness and honesty
- Care and consideration for others
- Self-discipline

Rights implicit in such a set of values would include:

- The right to be safe
- The right to a fair hearing
- The right to be heard
- The right to be treated with respect
- The right to be able to teach and learn without unnecessary disruption

It must be noted that rights for anyone cannot exist in a vacuum. They can only be afforded if the members of the school community also take responsibility for their actions. Responsibilities included in any school handbook on behaviour might encompass:

- Allowing other pupils get on with their work.
- Sorting out disagreements in a non-violent way

For teachers responsibilities might include:

- The provision of appropriate work for all students
- To treat all pupils with respect and fairness

Rules

> .... whole-school rules should be few in number and sensible in their implementation. They must be seen to be fair, both to children and staff, allowing equal opportunity for all to succeed, and they must change and develop in response to the changing needs of the children.
>
> *Stone (1990, p.116)*

Research indicates the many systems, methods and policies available to schools seeking to regulate behaviour. These vary in style and emphasis but are often distinguished in the following ways:

- sanctions versus rewards
- coercive versus relational
- spirit of intervention rather than the letter of the law
- autocratic versus democratic

The range of behaviour policies is huge with advocates of the autocratic approach looking for schools to develop "strict, clearly delineated disciplinary codes and enforcement – a list of dos and don't and the penalties for disobedience". (Gordon, 1999, p.1) There are many voices in opposition to an authoritarian code of discipline including Kohn (1996), as cited by Gordon (1999, p.3): "This matter-of-fact demand for mindless obedience follows quite naturally from the premise that all problems are the students' fault". It often appears that autocratic modes of behaviour modification are fruitless since they do not relieve the fear, distrust, verbal threats, and physical pain many children bring to school. (Schreiber Dill and Haberman, 1995)

We need to look at why we have the rules we have and whether they are appropriate. Too often rules exist in a school "because of tradition and ritual rather than because they promote or encourage an effective school". (Hansen and Childs, 1998, p.16) We need to involve the pupils not only in drawing up the rules but also in explaining why a particular rule is necessary. This can only have a positive impact on behaviour in schools since "children who not only know the rules but were involved in drawing them up are more likely to respect them – and can't complain about things not being fair when they are punished for infringing them. (Klein, 1999, p.143)

A Role for Rules – The Need for Logical Consequences

Rules are effective when they are:

- Few in number
- Reasonable & fair
- Explained, discussed with & taught to pupils
- Simple & precise
- Enforced and enforceable
- Positive – they should describe the behaviours the school wants to see

Rules should address:

- The way people treat each other
- The resolution of difficulties & conflicts
- Noise, movement & safety around the school
- How pupils get teacher's attention

Consequences are required:

- To encourage pupils to recognise that their actions have logical effect on others
- To encourage an awareness of personal choice around behaviour and the notion of taking responsibility for one's actions
- To try to build and maintain a positive relationship

Why Emphasise the Positive?

Discipline that is synonymous with punishment, as is still the case in many schools, only focuses on misbehaviour. It places huge pressures on teachers and students since the expectation remains that students are inherently bad and cannot develop self-discipline. Using a strict disciplinarian means of modifying student behaviour may prove pointless since punishments "often serve only to help prevent a behaviour occurring in the future; by themselves they do not provide alternative acceptable behaviours which should be used". Charlton and David (1993, p.211) Many schools, whether their approach is autocratic or democratic, have adopted some form of discipline code that incorporates sanctions and rewards. There are issues surrounding the use of both and they must be used carefully.

The role of sanctions

> Good discipline certainly requires that our students experience the consequences of their misbehaviour, but that is only one aspect of the process.
>
> *Gootman (1997, p.2)*

There is a need for guidelines, for students to know the boundaries in terms of appropriate behaviour. Advocates of the various democratic approaches to developing behaviour policies do not deny this. Instead, they suggest that "children will behave if teachers give them more positive reinforcement and decision making authority, and offer them more engaging curricula. (Gordon 1999, p.1) The most successful behaviour management programmes are those which allow the student to learn from their mistakes and make choices about behaviour rather than stopping the poor behaviour simply to have an easier life. They seem to emphasise the use of rewards along with sanctions. The involvement of students and parents in the process is key, and that involvement must be genuine, allowing students and parents real say in the rules, the sanctions and the rewards. According to Gordon (1999, p.2) "Involving students in the process doesn't mean throwing out the rule book" though unfortunately that is what many teachers and school managers fear will happen if students are allowed a say in drawing up the behaviour code. What is clear is that any policy should evolve through community agreement with each member of the school having his/her say. As Kavanagh (1993, pp.67-68) asserts "the notion of a school receiving a 'code of discipline' from some outside source is out of harmony with the recommendations of research and experience". He goes on to point out, realistically, that top-down measures or policies enforced by the Department "are not likely to impinge, in any appreciable manner, on the myriad staff-student interactions which comprise the ordinary routine of school".

Whatever sanctions are used, and we must recognise that they are a necessary part of teaching students responsibility, they should be drawn up so that they are what Gootman (1997) refers to as logical, child accountable and leave dignity intact. In terms of sanctions the emphasis for the future will have to be a move away from suspension and expulsion towards more in-house strategies. Withdrawal from school activities while remaining on the premises can be very useful, particularly for serious incidents. It has the following advantages;

- The student has the opportunity to cool down and reflect on their own behaviour

- It ensures that the duty of care is maintained

- It allows for teaching and learning to continue without interference

- It provides an opportunity for negotiation

Students can be withdrawn from

- One or more supervised subjects

- Break and lunch with peers – supervised alternatives must be provided

- School activities or extra-curricular programmes

Other suitable sanctions include placement of the student on a Conduct Card/Behaviour Monitoring Sheet for a period of time. This allows for monitoring and modification of specific behavioural problems associated with a student. It also provides for recognition of success and acknowledgement of improvement where appropriate. Some schools also use Class monitoring sheets or books. Student contracts are favoured by some schools, particularly for students returning after suspension or entering the school with a history of misbehaviour. The legal standing of such contracts might be questionable in the future as the full implications. Sample materials such as Conduct Card and Behaviour Think sheet are included in Section Seven.

The role of rewards

The problem with several of the behaviour management policies which emphasise reward and 'catching a student being good' is that it may be difficult to reward some individuals. If the rewards are made untruthfully then students will be the first to recognise that. "Dishonest praise discourages children as well as adults and can be damaging to their self-esteem. The intentions of the praiser do not matter. What matters is how the child feels as a result of the praise". (Gootman, 1997, p.47) Where rewards are used the school needs too look at whether or not they make sense. Could students interpret any given reward as a bribe and perform accordingly, not through any desire to improve behaviour but simply to please the teacher enough to win the prize. In addition, using rewards to modify behaviour often creates the kind of competitive culture schools should be trying to move away from. The ideal would appear to be a reward system that can be designed without setting up sharp competition between pupils. This minimises conflict but is not easy to do since "too many rewards end up robbing children of the desire to do something because they know inside that it's the right thing to do". (Gootman, 1997, p.56) The key factor in the actual design of any behaviour management policy is that it is appropriate for the context of the school and meets the needs of all members of the school community. There is much evidence that "when sanctions are used against a background of high expectations, positive reinforcement for efforts made and clear indications that each child is a valued member of the school, no matter what his particular problems, there is a chance of their being meaningful". (Stone, 1990, p.117)

Some examples of appropriate awards are outlined below.

INDIVIDUAL REWARDS

Positive written comment in homework diary/specially designed letters/postcards

Verbal praise from teacher

Positive comment to tutor/class teacher/ Year Head

Credit system – positive stickers/stamps in journal

Record of achievement

Lunch time T.V. or music

Student of the month – Best academic/Most improved

Overall contribution/Student of the year

Photographs of award winners taken & displayed

CLASS REWARDS

Reduced homework on an agreed night

Subject related games

Positive comment to tutor/Year Head/Deputy Principal

Educational trips & outdoor activities

Class prizes

Work exhibited

Videos

Reward assemblies

Where a rewards or awards scheme has already been put in place the outcomes need to be monitored closely in order to judge its rate of success in reducing misbehaviour. Obviously one method of evaluating the system is to assess the number of referrals and compare with previous terms or years. However, it is also important to ask student how they feel about the scheme and whether they feel any changes are necessary. They may have some very useful suggestions.

One such format might be to use tutor time/registration or SPHE class to ask students the following questions:

1. **Rate how highly you value the rewards available within the current system.**

2. **Compile a list of your own 5 'ideal' rewards. Remember that there are financial and other constraints so be realistic!**

3. **How many rewards have you won since the system began?**

4. **How do you feel about the reward system in general?**

Use of Support Services

Where all of the rewards and sanctions available to the school bring about no improvement in a student's behaviour there may be a need for use of the support services available. However, it is worth noting the following:

- support services have limited resources – they have to concentrate on the most severe cases

- by the time the support service is involved the pupil may have been excluded or has become so disaffected he/she has dropped out

- schools are frustrated and lose faith when there is such a backlog

- the support service may become a vehicle to get kids out

Sample Code of Behaviour – Primary Level

The following Draft Code of Behaviour was drawn up by the staff of Everyman Primary School. It was presented to the Parents Council in draft form. Their observations and comments were presented along with the draft policy to the Board of Management. The Policy was ratified by the Board.

It will be circulated to all parents in September.

This policy was formulated in accordance with the Education Act 1998, Section 15, (1), (2) Section 21. (1), (3), (4), Section 23, (2)(3) and in accordance with Circular 20/90 of the Dept. of Education and Rule 130 of the 'Rules for National Schools' of the Dept. of Education, especially section (3) 'The use of corporal punishment is forbidden'.

This code of discipline is based on reward as well as on compliance and sanction. For very serious misbehaviour parents will be asked to meet with either a disciplinary committee or with the Board of Management.

The emphasis in the school is on promoting good behaviour rather than on punishing bad. For the most part it is trouble free. At the same time it is no harm that parents are aware of the procedures used in the school and work with the school in ensuring that all children are happy at school.

The aims of our Code of Behaviour are:

♦ To allow for the smooth and effective running of the school.

♦ To enhance the learning environment of the school by promoting a sense of mutual respect among all members of the school community.

♦ To ensure consistency in the application of rules and sanctions.

♦ To facilitate the development and education of all children.

♦ To increase the co-operation between home and school.

♦ To outline the structure of fair and agreed sanctions that will be available to teachers in response to negative behaviour.

♦ To promote equality and fairness for all.

♦ To promote good behaviour and self-discipline among the children.

♦ To promote the safety and happiness of all children and staff in the school.

Code of Behaviour

Rather than listing all the possible behaviours that might be unacceptable there are instead clear definitions of the differing roles and expectations of the people involved in the everyday life of the school.

Expectations in this school

The school expects that you will:	Your teacher expects that you will:
• Attend school regularly and not miss days without good reason • Arrive on time. • Not leave during the day without permission • Respect all school property • Wear the school uniform • Show respect for yourself and others • Avoid swearing, fighting or name-calling. • Listen to messages given and do as requested. • Participate in school activities • Move quietly around the school and avoid causing disturbance. • Keep the school tidy and litter-free.	• Show him/her courtesy and respect • Accept his/her authority and responsibility and his/her right to teach and impose sanctions on those who behave badly. • Come to school on time and have all the necessary materials. • Do your homework carefully and completely. • Listen when others are talking. • Avoid distracting behaviour. • Participate in all class activities. • Follow the rules drawn up by your class.

Your fellow students expect that you will:	Children expect that school will be:
• Not bully them • Show acceptance and respect their differing personalities • Never insult or belittle them because of differences. • Respect their property • Listen to them and acknowledge them • Share equipment and resources with them • Allow them to be part of the group • Speak to them with courtesy and respect.	• Safe • Happy • Suited to their learning style • Encouraging and supportive. • Affirming of children of all abilities • Able to deal with bullying and supportive of victims • A place where teaching and learning are at the core of all we do.

Parents expect that there will be:	Teachers expect that there will be:
• A safe and happy environment for their child. • Recognition and provision for the individual differences of pupils • Support for children who need it. • Fairness and consistency in the way children are dealt with. • No labelling of their child. • An atmosphere of support and inclusion rather than criticism. • Contact at an early stage to inform them of any problems • A willingness to listen to their viewpoint. • Suggestions and support about problems in school.	• Mutual support and encouragement. • Co-operation to achieve the schools aims and objectives. • A fair and consistent implementation of the school discipline policy • A consistent approach to handling troubled children. • An atmosphere that encourages professional development and a willingness to learn and change.

Expectations of Parents:	Your child expects that you will:
The school expects that you will: • Be familiar with the various policies and codes of the school and the expectation of pupils. • Show support for teachers in their implementation of the schools behaviour policy. • Support your child in his schoolwork & ensure he has the necessary materials • Ensure the punctuality and regular attendance of your child. • Ensure your child has a positive attitude to and abides by the school and class rules. • Never undermine the authority of the school or teachers & promote respect for teachers and other school personnel. • Give a contact number where you can be reached in an emergency & be available to discuss a problem.	• Look after his basic needs • Be interested in, support, praise and encourage his work in school. • Show fairness. **Other parents expect that you will:** • Support the school in implementing its code of behaviour. • Exert firm discipline in cases where your child's behaviour is having a negative impact on the behaviour of others.

Responses and sanctions available to teachers and school:

In-class:	Final Phase:
• Quiet word • Special mention • Reminder of school or class rules • Short instruction • Seek an explanation • Ask child why he is doing it. • Change position in class. • Temporary isolation from group • Longer interview away from class group. • Loss of minor privileges • Note in homework journal./ Chat with parents • Lines (Signed / Small number)	• 2nd interview between parents and School Disciplinary Committee (Chairperson, Principal and Deputy-Principal) • Referral for assessment (if appropriate.) • If behaviour continues suspension is agreed by BOM. • Parents are notified of date and duration of suspension. • Parents should take responsibility to obtain and ensure the completion of all homework during the period of suspension. • Child returns with parent following suspension and a behavioural contract is agreed. • If behaviour continues then a 2nd (and longer) suspension is imposed. (Circular 20/90, Rule 130.) • If behaviour continues then the school should seek an alternative placement for the child or a further referral is made as appropriate. • For serious negative behaviour a child need not proceed through the various stages. Appropriate action can be taken by the Principal or by the Board of Management. • For serious confrontational behaviour the Principal may choose to contact parents immediately, or to leave a child home. • The child will return with a parent the following day and a behavioural contract will be agreed.
Next Phase	
• Send to another class • Referral to principal • Yellow Card (Parents are informed by post of problem behaviour in the school) • 2nd Yellow Card • Following two yellow cards in a term a **Red Card** will be sent home. Parents come to school to discuss problem with teacher *and principal, if appropriate*)	

Sample Code of Behaviour – Secondary Level

1. General Philosophy

The philosophy of the Behaviour Policy of St. Sophie's School is embodied in the Code of Conduct, which was drawn up in conjunction with students, parents and staff.

Code of Conduct

Treat everyone at school with care and respect
Take good care of our school
Call others by their proper names
Keep your hands and feet to yourself
Be careful with others' property
Always walk quietly and sensibly around school

Care of school premises and sites

Everyone in the school is responsible for the care of the school premises.

Students and staff are encouraged to feel a sense of ownership for the school and its environment.

- Staff will display student's work.
- The building will be kept clean and tidy.
- The grounds will be kept free of litter.

2. Aims of the Policy

To develop a moral framework within which initiative, responsibility and sound relationships can flourish;

To enable students to develop a sense of self worth and a respect and tolerance for others;

To produce an environment in which students feel safe, secure and respected.

3. Objectives

For students to show:

- self confidence;

- self control;
- sensitivity and consideration for others;
- a pride in themselves and their school;
- an interest in their activities.

For students to develop:

- responsibility for their learning and their environment;
- an independence of mind;
- a sense of fairness;
- an understanding of the need for rules;
- a respect and tolerance for others' ways of life and different opinions;
- non sexist attitudes;
- non racist attitudes;
- a persistent approach to tasks;
- an acceptable reaction to bullying and abuse.

4. A Positive Focus

Students' achievements, academic or otherwise, will be recognised.

Rewards will be accessible to all students.

Assembly will be used as an opportunity to acknowledge achievements and to foster a sense of community.

Students will be encouraged to share their achievement with a senior member of staff, their parents and other children.

Examples of students' work and achievements will be displayed in the classrooms and around the school

5. Unacceptable Behaviour

Unacceptable behaviour includes:

- disobedience;
- biting, spitting, hitting and kicking;
- foul language and swearing;
- making unkind remarks;
- damaging property;
- answering back, rudeness or aggression to adults;
- stealing;
- truancy;
- bullying

6. Sanctions

A firm reprimand from a member of staff is expected to be sufficient to correct inappropriate behaviour. However, if this fails to correct the behaviour of a student the following procedures may be adopted:

In the classroom

Time out – removal from the scene of an incident. This may mean:

- working at a different place,
- working in another classroom by arrangement with the class teacher,
- working in the corridor outside the principal's office by prior arrangement.

In the schoolyard/on the corridor

A student is taken indoors for a five minute cooling off period.

A community task – e.g. picking up litter, tidying a shelf or cupboard.

If the above sanctions do not lead to a modification of behaviour, the following may be considered.

- Exclusion from a favoured activity – this must be immediate, but can only be used occasionally. It has to be considered whether it is educationally sound to deprive students of particular lessons. They cannot learn to behave in lessons if they are removed from them.
- Exclusion from the right to represent the school. This sanction should be used only rarely.
- The establishment of a behaviour record.
- A verbal disciplining from senior member of staff – Principal, Deputy Principal or Year Head.
- A requirement for a written apology.
- A regular report to be given to the principal.
- A letter/telephone call to a parent from the principal.
- A meeting with parent(s).
- Other sanctions following discussion between parents, class teacher and principal.
- Exclusion from school (DES guidelines to be followed).

7. Racist/Offensive remarks

- A student is reprimanded and record of the incident kept.
- For a repeated offence, a record is kept and parents informed.
- In persistent cases, parents may be asked to discuss the matter with the principal.

8. Rewards

Rewards for good behaviour include:

- praise from staff;
- responsibilities given;
- quality time in the classroom when good work and good behaviour are acknowledged;
- showing good work to the principal;
- showing good work in school assembly;
- showing work at choosing time at the end of the week;
- the use of stars – individual staff may wish to award stars for merit and do so at their discretion.

9. Parents

Parents have a vital role in promoting good behaviour in school and so effective home/school liaison is very important. The school has a right to expect that parents will give their full support in dealing with their child's behaviour.

We expect Parents:

- to keep us informed of behaviour difficulties they may be experiencing at home;
- inform us of any trauma which may affect their child's performance or behaviour at school e.g. a death in the family;
- inform us about their child's ill health and any absences connected with it.

The school will endeavour to achieve good home/school liaison by:

- promoting a welcoming environment within the school;
- giving parents regular constructive and positive comment on their child's work and behaviour;
- encouraging parents to come into school on occasions other than parents' evenings;
- keeping parent informed of school activities by letter, newsletter etc;
- involving parents at an early stage in any disciplinary problems.

10. Other Agencies

Full use will be made of such agencies as Education Welfare Officers, Social Services, Health Services and the Educational Psychological Services where appropriate.

Rules About Rules

- THE RULES MUST BE EXPRESSED POSITIVELY – to convey the expectation that students will behave well

- THE RATIONALE FOR THOSE RULES MUST BE SPELT OUT – we must not take for granted that students will understand why rules are necessary.

- THE RULES MUST BE ESSENTIAL – are there so many rules that their significance is lost?

- THE RULES NEED TO BE DECIDED UPON BY THE SCHOOL AS A COMMUNITY

KEY QUESTIONS FOR SCHOOLS

❏ **Are OUR rules framed positively?**

❏ **Do WE spell out to students the reasoning behind the rules?**

❏ **Do OUR rules encourage self-responsibility?**

❏ **Do WE reject the behaviour, not the student?**

❏ **Have WE established a secure and caring environment for all?**

Information Sheet

KEY QUESTIONS FOR SCHOOLS

Transmitting The Positive Message – Are Our Sanctions 'Sane'?

❏ Are the rules framed positively?

❏ Are all the rules essential?

❏ Can we justify each rule?

❏ Are there so many rules that their impact on students is minimal?

❏ Is the rationale for the rules obvious to everyone in the school community?

❏ Have the rules been decided by the school as a community?

❏ Are the rules we have on paper really those we use in practice?

❏ What do the sanctions we use convey?

❏ Are the sanctions intended to minimise disruption to learning for the offender?

❏ Are they intended to let everyone know that the student has misbehaved?

❏ Do we reject behaviour and not the person?

❏ Have we established a secure and caring environment for everyone in the school community?

❏ Do the sanctions punish the teacher because they involve extra work?

❏ Is there consistent use of sanctions across the school?

❏ Does the punishment fit the crime?

YOU MAY PHOTOCOPY THIS PAGE

SECTION SIX

AUDIT MATERIALS

Introduction

The materials which follow are designed for use by schools engaged in a process of review and development of whole school behaviour policy. They provide stimuli for discussion and reflection and aim to seek out the views of all members of the school community – teachers, management, students and parents.

Current Practices Around Behaviour

Answer the questions below individually, then join your assigned group to discuss the issues which have arisen.

What is working well at the moment?	What are we meant to do but need to tighten up on?
What could we do without too much planning?	**What should we plan for the medium/ long term?**

WHOLE SCHOOL BEHAVIOUR POLICY

TEACHER QUESTIONNAIRE – AWARENESS

Please give your opinions on our school's behaviour policy by ticking the boxes below. Fell free to add any comments you feel are important.

		True	Untrue	Comment
1	I am clear about the philosophy underpinning our behaviour code.			
2	I am clear about the reward and sanction system in operation.			
3	I am clear about the ladder of referral written into our code.			
4	I am clear that students understand the school's expectations of them in terms of behaviour.			
5	I often give rewards to students for good or improved behaviour and other aspects of school life, as well as for academic success.			
6	I have a role in rewarding good behaviour outside of class.			
7	I have a role in sanctioning poor behaviour that takes place outside class.			
8	The school behaviour policy informs my classroom practices.			
9	I feel a sense of ownership of the behaviour policy.			
10	I have had opportunities to identify my needs for professional development around behaviour management.			
11	My need for professional development around behaviour issues has been met.			
12	In our school there is support available in relation to students with challenging behaviour.			
13	I treat students as I expect to be treated.			
14	I make an effort to listen to students and to get to know them as individuals.			
15	I am conscious of how I can affect students' self-esteem.			
16	I consult students regularly and believe they have important and useful things to say.			
17	I spend time teaching students about the behavioural expectations of this school.			
18	I try to encourage students to take responsibility for their own behaviour.			
19	I try to model the behaviour I would like to see in all students.			
20	I have high expectations of all students irrespective of academic ability.			

Please include any additional comments you feel might be useful:

YOU MAY PHOTOCOPY THIS PAGE

TEACHER PERCEPTIONS OF STUDENT NEEDS

The following 8 statements express student opinions about their needs in terms of teaching and schooling. Read the statements & decide whether you agree or disagree with each statement. Where possible include a reason for your answer in the space beneath the statement.

	AGREE	DISAGREE
Students want to be trusted and respected.		
Students want to be part of a family.		
Students want teachers to be helpers.		
Students want opportunities to be responsible.		
Students want freedom, not license.		
Students want a place where people care.		
Students want teachers who help them succeed, not fail.		
Students want to have choices.		

YOU MAY PHOTOCOPY THIS PAGE

QUESTIONNAIRE FOR SENIOR MANAGEMENT

These questions are designed for self-reflection around the issue of behaviour management. Please answer the questions by ticking the boxes.

	YES	NO
Are you seen around potential trouble spots?		
Are you involved in dealing with indiscipline both in classrooms and on the corridors, in the yard etc?		
Do you feel you balance your time between dealing with disruption and actively promoting positive behaviour?		
Do you give feedback to staff on discipline issues?		
Do pupils know what is expected of them in terms of behaviour?		
Do you monitor patterns of misbehaviour, e.g. kinds of offences, age group involved etc.?		
Do you monitor the effectiveness of your current system?		
Does the school have a plan for training new staff in important procedures like the behaviour system?		
Is there a mentoring system for new teachers?		
Does the school celebrate the achievement and successes of all students?		
Does positive recognition share the same status as sanctions and punishment?		
Does the school share positive news about students with parents and the wider community?		
Can parents and students have a part in reviewing current practices and developing new ones?		
Does the school attempt to encourage students to manage their own behaviour?		
Are there specific interventions for those students who have severe difficulty in following behaviour procedures?		

YOU MAY PHOTOCOPY THIS PAGE

STUDENT QUESTIONNAIRE – SAMPLE 1

This survey is about how you see your school in terms of discipline, how you see yourself in terms of behaviour and asking for help. You don't have to give your name. The answers you give will be confidential. Nobody will know what any individual said. Don't fill in anything you don't want to but please be honest about what you do fill in. For each statement tick the box which you feel represents your opinion.

What year are you in: [   ]

In our school, rules about behaviour are posted and everyone knows them	Absolutely true	Usually true	More or less true	Not very true	Not true at all
In our school, there are rewards for good behaviour and everyone gets the same ones	Absolutely true	Usually true	More or less true	Not very true	Not true at all
In our school, there is variation among teachers about how much they stick to the rules	Absolutely true	Usually true	More or less true	Not very true	Not true at all
In our school, sexual harassment	Never happens	Rarely happens	Sometimes happens	Often happens	Happens all the time
In our school, racial slurs and conflict	Never happens	Rarely happens	Sometimes happens	Often happens	Happens all the time
In our school, some kids feel left out	Never happens	Rarely happens	Sometimes happens	Often happens	Happens all the time
In our school, students show respect to teachers	All the time	Most of the time	Sometimes	Not usually	Hardly ever
In our school, teachers show respect to students	All the time	Most of the time	Sometimes	Not usually	Hardly ever
In our school, swearing or cursing is	Never allowed	Not allowed in class	Discouraged but not punished	Ignored	Encouraged
In our school, I have seen people smoke tobacco	Never	Once	Sometimes	Frequently	Every day
In our school, I have used tobacco on school grounds	Never	Once	Sometimes	Frequently	Every day
In our school, I have seen people vandalising or defacing school property	Never	Once	Two or three times	Four to ten times	More than ten times

In our school, I have vandalised or defaced school property	Never	Once	Two or three times	Four to ten times	More than ten times
I have the skills I need to deal with life's problems	Describes me very well	Describes me pretty well	Sometimes describes me	Does not really describe me	Does not describe me at all
I am able to control my anger even when I am upset	Describes me very well	Describes me pretty well	Sometimes describes me	Does not really describe me	Does not describe me at all
I am able to deal with uncomfortable feelings like anger, embarrassment or sadness	Describes me very well	Describes me pretty well	Sometimes describes me	Does not really describe me	Does not describe me at all
I am able to stand up for myself and can do so without fighting	Describes me very well	Describes me pretty well	Sometimes describes me	Does not really describe me	Does not describe me at all
I think of the consequences before I act	Describes me very well	Describes me pretty well	Sometimes describes me	Does not really describe me	Does not describe me at all
If I have a problem I talk to my parents	Almost always	Usually	Sometimes	Not often	Almost never
If I have a problem I talk to my friends	Almost always	Usually	Sometimes	Not often	Almost never
If I have a problem I talk to a teacher	Almost always	Usually	Sometimes	Not often	Almost never
If I have a problem I talk to the guidance counsellor	Almost always	Usually	Sometimes	Not often	Almost never
If I have a problem I keep it to myself	Almost always	Usually	Sometimes	Not often	Almost never
I would go to an adult if my safety or the safety of others was at risk	Almost always	Usually	Sometimes	Not often	Almost never

63

WHOLE SCHOOL BEHAVIOUR POLICY - AWARENESS
STUDENT QUESTIONNAIRE – SAMPLE 2

Year Group:

Please fill in the grid below and add any comments you feel are important.

		True	Untrue	Comment
1	I know how the school rewards good behaviour and work			
2	I know what punishments there are for poor behaviour and work			
3	I know who I will have to see if my behaviour is not good			
4	I know when my parents will be informed & involved if my behaviour is not good			
5	I know how I am expected to behave in this school			
6	All the teachers at this school give the same amount of rewards & punishments			
7	Rewards are given for behaviour as well as for good work			
8	The rewards given at this school make me want to behave and work hard			What rewards do you like best? What other rewards would make students want to behave well and work hard?
9	The consequences of misbehaving used in this school stop me from behaving badly			What consequences are the most useful in stopping pupils' misbehaviour?

	True	Untrue	Comment
10 All staff are involved in rewarding good behaviour outside of class			
11 All staff give punishment if they see poor behaviour outside class			
12 I have space to keep my belongings			
13 I have somewhere safe to go at break time or lunchtime			
14 There are no areas within the school grounds that I do not feel safe in			If there are areas in which you do not feel safe, please say where they are:
15 Lessons are about the right length for me			
16 My behaviour is the same for all subjects			If you behave worse in some groups/subjects than others, can you say why you think this is?
17 I have the opportunity to say what I feel about the school rules, rewards and punishments			
18 My parents/guardians have received more good letters or phone calls about my behaviour than bad ones			
19 Adults in this school treat me as they expect to be treated			
20 Adults in this school listen to me and get to know me as an individual			
21 Adults are careful not to make me feel bad			
22 I feel that adults in this school ask my opinion and feel I have something important to say			
23 Assemblies, year group and class meetings are used to discuss behaviour and celebrate positive behaviour			
24 Teachers teach me the school's expectations and remind me when I forget			
25 I have the opportunity to learn about dealing with my feelings, resolving conflict, being assertive, bullying etc. in some classes			

STUDENT QUESTIONNAIRE – SAMPLE 3

STUDENT PERCEPTIONS ON BEHAVIOUR

Please rate the following statements about behaviour as very important, fairly important, not really important for you to get on well in your everyday life at school.

Please tick one box for each statement.

	Very important	Fairly important	Not important
Being helpful			
Being responsible			
Being friendly			
Being nice to others			
Not eating in class			
Behaving when the teacher has to leave the classroom			
Listening to the teacher			
Remembering your equipment (pens, copies, books etc.)			
Working hard			
Not talking in class			
Being organised			
Arriving on time			
Staying in your seat			
Co-operating with the teacher			
Co-operating with others			

Which of these is most likely or unlikely to encourage a change in your behaviour? Please tick one box for each statement.

	Most likely	Possibly	Unlikely
Teachers mentioning good things you have done			
Getting rewards for being well behaved			
The threat of detention			
The school contacting your parents			
Being given extra work as punishment			
Doing interesting work in class			
Being treated with respect			
Teachers pointing out bad things you have done			
Having privileges withdrawn for misbehaviour, e.g. being dropped from a team			
The class being rewarded for good behaviour			
Having a night off homework			
Being allowed to choose an activity			

STUDENT SURVEY – SAMPLE 4

For use after the introduction of an awards/rewards scheme

1. Are you happy with the current awards scheme in operation in the school?

   Please circle your answer.   **Yes   No**

2. If you said you are unhappy with the current scheme please give the main reason for your answer.

   _____

3. If you are happy for the scheme to continue as it is now, what is your main reason?

   _____

4. Since the start of the scheme have you noticed any of the following in your classes:

	True	Untrue
The class tried to behave or behaved better		
The class was able to work more efficiently and learn more		
The class enjoyed gaining a reward or positive feedback		
The class enjoyed the subject more		
The class didn't get shouted at		
The class didn't get into trouble		
Students learned how teachers expected them to behave		
School was more enjoyable		

5. Do you think any of the suggestions listed below would help improve the scheme?

	True	Untrue
Some form of prize (e.g. best pupil/best class)		
More frequent rewards		
Involve classes more in making decisions about the scheme		
Points for attendance		
Fewer rules		
Less strict rules		
Make it more fun		
Have pupils involved in deciding who deserves the prizes		

6. What other ways do you think the scheme could be improved?

   _____

   _____

   _____

7. Can you suggest targets for the behaviour scheme for next term?

   _____

   _____

   _____

YOU MAY PHOTOCOPY THIS PAGE

WHOLE SCHOOL BEHAVIOUR POLICY
PARENT QUESTIONNAIRE – AWARENESS

Please give your opinions on our school's behaviour policy by ticking the boxes below. Fell free to add any comments you feel are important.

		True	Untrue	Comment
1	I understand why the school does what it does to promote positive behaviour.			
2	I know what rewards me child will get if he/she behaves well and works hard.			
3	I know what punishment children get if they do not behave well or work hard.			
4	I am clear about what the school expects from my child in terms of behaviour.			
5	My child can receive rewards for good behaviour and other aspects of school life, as well as for good work.			
6	The school treats me as a partner in my child's education.			
7	I have received more good letters and phone calls about my child's behaviour than bad ones.			
8	The school listens to my child and gets to know him/her as an individual.			
9	If a child needs to improve on behaviour the school helps him/her do so in a positive way.			
10	Adults behave in the way they would like the pupils to behave.			
11	If my child needs extra academic help the school provides it.			
12	The school is welcoming to students and parents.			

Please include any additional comments you would like to add:

PROMOTING POSITIVE BEHAVIOUR
Parental Opinions

This school is hoping to introduce a new whole-school behaviour management policy. Please tick you responses to the following as useful methods of promoting positive behaviour:

	Most useful	Unsure	Not useful
Awarding points to individuals for good behaviour.			
Awarding points to class groups for good behaviour			
Setting clear targets for behaviour.			
Discussing what good behaviour is.			
Rewarding good behaviour with certificates			
Letting parents know by phone or through journal when student has behaved well			
Setting targets for pupils with difficulties			
Providing additional support for pupils in difficulty			
Providing alternative classwork for pupils who need it			
Teaching behaviour in the same way as academic subjects are taught			

We are keen to know what you feel are effective ways of dealing with your children should they misbehave. Please tick your responses to what is likely to encourage your child not to misbehave again.

	Most likely	Possibly	Unlikely
Teachers mentioning good things they have done			
Getting rewards for being well behaved			
The threat of detention			
The school contacting parents			
Being given extra work as punishment			
Doing interesting work in class			
Being treated with respect			
Teachers pointing out bad things they have done			
Having privileges withdrawn for misbehaviour, e.g. being dropped from a team			
The class being rewarded for good behaviour			
Having a night off homework			
Being allowed to choose an activity			

YOU MAY PHOTOCOPY THIS PAGE

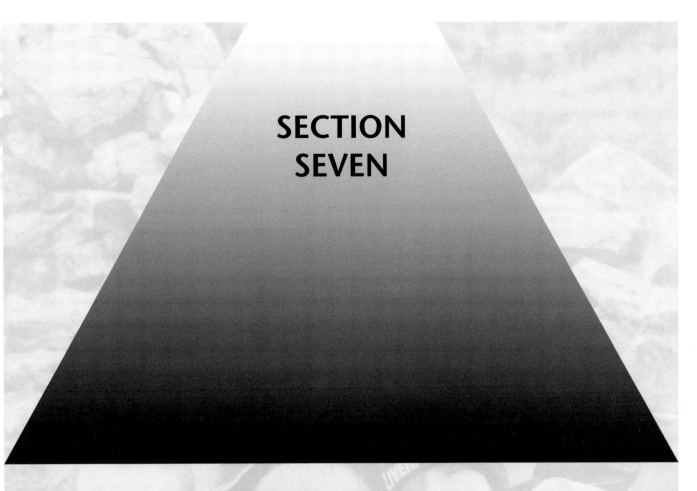

SECTION
SEVEN

IDEAS BANK

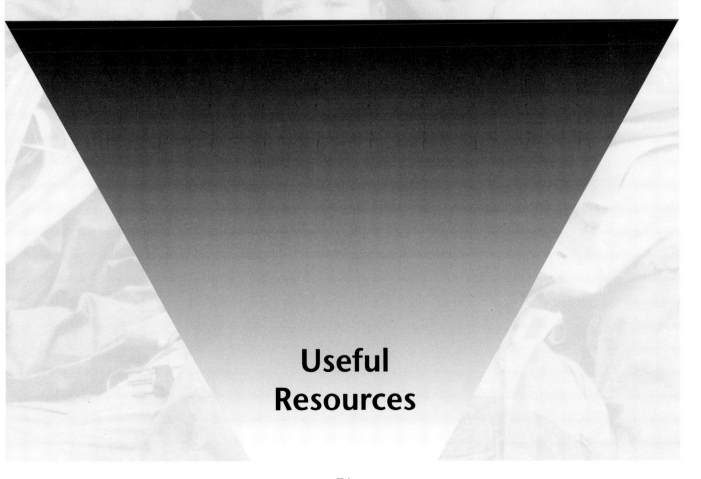

Useful
Resources

Introduction

The materials in this section have been developed as suggested responses to behavioural issues. They would have to be adapted for a school's particular needs and individual context.

PREVENTION: The posters, information sheets and forms are designed to provide ideas in terms of creating a positive climate and building relationships which focus on high expectations and care. In some cases they are designed to put the onus on the student to take responsibility for his/ her own learning and behaviour, e.g. Homework Excuse Note/Missing Assignment Reminder. Others are simply intended to help create an atmosphere where positive behaviour is the norm. There are also a number of forms designed to help with teachers' record keeping and the organisational aspects of classroom management.

INTERVENTION: Since students are no more perfect than teachers we can assume that some will make mistakes and misbehave despite our best efforts! The worksheets and exercises that follow are designed to let the student think about behaviour. Again the emphasis is on taking responsibility. They work well when time has been spent explaining and teaching the rules and consequences of the Code of Behaviour to students, acting as a more meaningful and thought-provoking sanction than lines or other punishment exercises.

POSTVENTION: For some students ongoing help in the form of behaviour plans or record sheets will be necessary. Samples of such forms are included in this section.

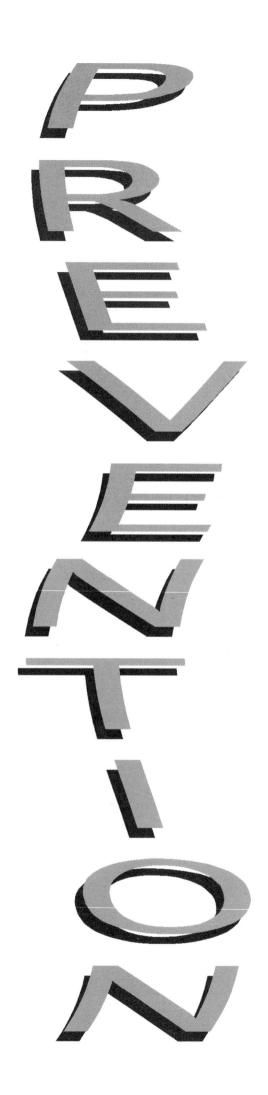

POSITIVE WAYS OF BUILDING STUDENT SELF-ESTEEM
AND RELATIONSHIP WITH SCHOOL

These are in operation in many of our schools and can only enhance the relationships that are at the heart of behaviour management.

- Word/Trait/Slogan of the Week/Month

- Use of intercom to make positive announcements each morning

- Posters

- Themed assemblies

- Use of awards and prizes

- Contests – e.g. tidy classroom

- Recognition wall for student achievement/use of photographs

- Displays of student work

- Peer mentoring, e.g., 5th Years to buddy 1st years

- Cross-age tutoring

- Community service projects, e.g., Edmund Rice Awards

- Charity fundraisers

- Student designed school materials, e.g. Christmas cards, bookmarks, calenders, T-shirts, 'Good news' postcards for use by teachers & Principal etc.

- School mural designed & painted by students

- Coat of arms creations

- Student council

- School clubs, sports, band, choir, drama etc.

- Newsletters/Yearbook

50 OPPORTUNITIES TO ACKNOWLEDGE GOOD BEHAVIOUR
AND PRAISE STUDENTS

Adapted from Canter's 'Assertive Discipline' Programme

1. entering the classroom quietly	26. good effort on a long-term project
2. putting away coat and bag	27. sharing
3. returning permission slips & forms on time	28. being sensitive to others' feelings
4. co-operating while teacher takes attendance	29. learning a new skill
5. being ready to work – having all equipment	30. appropriate use of school property
6. following directions	31. returning borrowed books and materials intact
7. saying please & thank you	32. showing enthusiasm/participating in school life
8. listening attentively	33. being responsible for a classroom job
9. helping a classmate	34. offering help without being asked
10. lining up	35. not wasting paper or other supplies
11. handing up homework on time	36. staying on task in group/individual work
12. being a good audience in assembly	37. telling the truth
13. beginning work quickly	38. accepting a new challenge
14. asking questions when unsure	39. behaving when a guest is in the classroom
15. good behaviour during a test	40. reading at home
16. participating in class discussions	41. participating in school functions
17. walking in corridors	42. demonstrating a positive attitude
18. working co-operatively with partner	43. giving one's best efforts
19. good behaviour on out-of-school activities	44. returning from the yard/lunch quietly
20. cleaning up	45. participating in group activities
21. good effort on a project/piece of homework	46. using problem-solving skills
22. helping a new student	47. showing creativity
23. sharing school experiences with parents	48. keeping busy when own work is finished
24. catching up on work after absence	49. taking turns
25. making new friends	50. helping younger student

CHOOSE RIGHT

FROM WRONG

STOP WHAT YOU ARE DOING

THINK ABOUT THE CONSEQUENCES

DO THE RIGHT THING!

EQUIP YOUR MIND

It's not the
size of the dog
in the fight
that matters
but the size
of the fight
in the
dog!

Star of the Week

ALL ABOUT ME

My favourite colour is

My favourite book is

My favourite movie is

My favourite sport is

When I grow up I want to be

I'm special because

I was born in

My favourite food is

I have a pet

The person I most admire is

My favourite school subject is

**Please complete this form about your child and send it back to school.
This will help me get to know your child. Thank you!**

Child's Name: _____

Name of parents or guardians: _____

Birthday: _____ Age _____ Phone No.: _____

My child is good at _____

_____

My child needs help with _____

_____

My child enjoys _____

My child likes to _____

_____

Academically, this year I would like to see my child work _____

_____

Socially, I would like to see my child work _____

_____

Anything else I should know about your child to help make the school year most successful?

_____

_____

Please return this form as quickly as possible.
Thank you for your participation in your child's education!

OUR CLASSROOM RULES

CONSEQUENCES

Equipment Checklist

Table Key: 1st line: Brought Materials (i.e. pens, copies, book)
2nd line: Took notes from board when required
3rd line: As needed: problems written, homework completed, etc

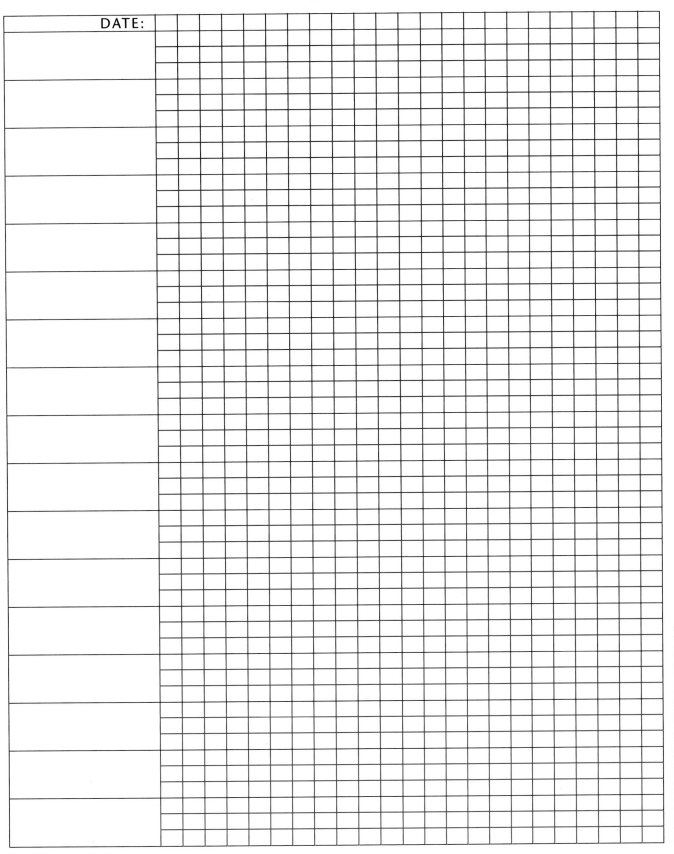

DATE:

GOOD NEWS!!

To: _____

Just to let you know that:

_____

_____

_____

_____

_____

Teacher: _____

Date: _____

HOMEWORK VOUCHER

To: _____

Just to let you know that:

_____

has been given a night off homework because:

_____

_____

_____

Teacher: _____

Date: _____

HOMEWORK EXCUSE

To: _____

Please outline why you did not complete: _____

Reason: _____

_____

_____

Student: _____

Teacher: _____

Date: _____

MISSING WORK

To: _____

Please take note that you are missing _____ assignments for my class.

Please complete the following:

_____

_____

_____

by: _____

Teacher: _____

Date: _____

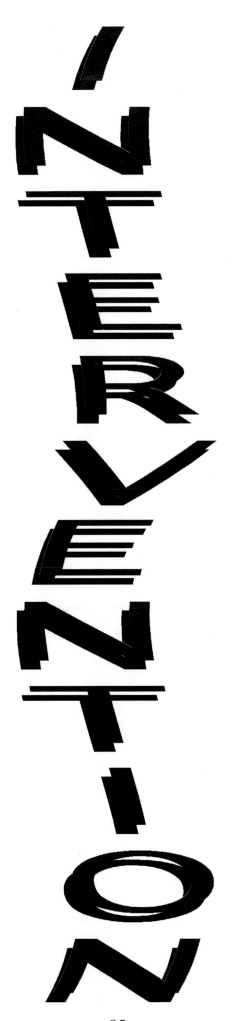

INTERVENTION

Behaviour Sheet

Name _____

Date _____

Time of Incident _____

This is the classroom rule I chose not to follow: _____

_____

_____

This is what happened: _____

_____

_____

_____

_____

This is why I did it: _____

_____

_____

_____

This is what I could have done: _____

_____

_____

_____

Teacher's Comments: _____

_____

_____

Other Comments: _____

_____

_____

Student Signature _____ **Date** _____

Teacher Signature _____ **Date** _____

Referral Form

Dear Teacher
Please complete this form and deliver it to the Principal's Office as soon as possible.

Student _____ Date _____ Time/Period _____

Please mark the principle(s) that were violated:

Respect

- [ ] Showing kindness
- [ ] Showing courtesy
- [ ] Showing tolerance
- [ ] Being fair

Responsibility

- [ ] Doing what's expected of him/her
- [ ] Doing what s/he promised s/he would do
- [ ] Taking responsibility for his/her actions
- [ ] Taking responsibility for the consequences of his/her actions
- [ ] Resisting negative peer pressure
- [ ] Telling the truth
- [ ] "Doing the right thing"

Safety

- [ ] Keeping him/herself safe
- [ ] Keeping the area safe for others

Please describe what happened before, during, and after the incident.
Describe the events in objective language that treats the student respectfully.
Describe how the principles identified above were violated.

Did you follow the referral procedure?   **Yes** [ ]   **No** [ ]

Student Response Form

Dear student

Please complete the following form. Please be respectful and honest in your words.

1. Describe what happened before, during, and after the incident. Tell what happened in the order that events occurred. Describe what each person did.

   _____

   _____

   _____

   _____

2. Please mark the principle(s) that the teacher believes that you violated:

   ## Respect

   ☐ Showing kindness

   ☐ Showing courtesy

   ☐ Showing tolerance

   ☐ Being fair

   ## Responsibility

   ☐ Doing what's expected of me

   ☐ Doing what I promised I would do

   ☐ Taking responsibility for my actions

   ☐ Taking responsibility for the consequences of my actions

   ☐ Resisting negative peer pressure

   ☐ Telling the truth

   ☐ "Doing the right thing"

   ## Safety

   ☐ Keeping myself safe

   ☐ Keeping the area safe for others

3. Did you violate the principle(s) at any time? (If so, please answer the following questions:) What wrong behaviour did you show? What did you want to accomplish with that behaviour?

   ☐ avoid work

   ☐ entertainment/fun

   ☐ impress other students

   ☐ get attention

   ☐ get revenge

   ☐ other (please write your reason)

How should you have acted in that situation?

_____

_____

_____

_____

_____

Please read the three items below and tell us how this situation can be resolved so that everyone has their dignity respected, and feels good about the outcome. Tell us how this situation can be prevented from happening again.

A. If you feel that the teacher was right when he or she sent you to the Principal, please suggest a fair and reasonable solution to this incident. What can you do to make things better?

_____

_____

_____

_____

_____

B. If you feel that you and the teacher were both wrong, please suggest a fair and reasonable solution to this incident. What can you and the teacher do to make things better?

_____

_____

_____

_____

_____

C. If you think that you have no fault in this incident, please suggest something that can prevent the situation from happening again. What can the teacher do to make things better? What can you do to help?

_____

_____

_____

_____

_____

All statements I have made on this form are truthful and honest

Signed: _____ **Date:** _____

Follow-up Form

Student name: _____

Date of referral/action: _____

Referring teacher: _____

I conducted an interview with the student identified above. The conversation covered the following points:

_____

_____

_____

_____

The student offered the following considerations in defence of his/her case:

_____

_____

_____

_____

Given the information gained from the interview and:

☐ the Principal's Referral Form

☐ the Student Response Form

☐ interviews/conversations with:

☐ other:

I have decided upon the following action:

_____

_____

_____

_____

☐ I need to speak with you as soon as possible.

☐ I do not need to speak with you at this time, but please contact me if you wish to discuss this
case further.

Signed: _____ **Date:** _____

THINKING ABOUT BEHAVIOUR LESSON

Answer the following questions in complete sentences, using most of the words in the question in your answer.

Please think carefully about your answers. The principal and/or your parents could read them in the near future.

1. What did you do that got you into trouble? _____

_____

_____

_____

_____

_____

_____

2. Why was it wrong to do what you did? _____

_____

_____

_____

_____

_____

_____

3. What can you do differently in the future so that you will not get into trouble?

_____

_____

_____

_____

_____

_____

4. What can the TEACHER do to help you stay out of trouble and to help you succeed in class?

_____

_____

_____

_____

_____

_____

Adapted from the work of the Harden Middle School

RESPECT LESSON

Please copy onto a separate piece of paper. Be sure to put your name in the right hand corner of your paper. Title your paper "Respect". After you have completed the assignment, place this sheet and your paper in the box.

We all need and deserve to be respected. However, we cannot respect others when we do not respect ourselves. When you are rude, put people down, talk negatively, or insult people, you are hurting your respect for yourself as well as for others.

Everyone needs to feel good about themselves in order to get along with others. When someone does not feel good about himself or herself, he or she speaks and acts in ways that hurts others. When you don't feel good about yourself, everyone loses.

We all have bad days. No one is immune to having things go wrong. That is why we always have to remember to treat people with respect, even if we are not feeling very good about ourselves, or can tell that they may not be feeling much respect for themselves. When you automatically treat people with respect, you help everyone feel better about themselves.

How can I treat people with respect automatically?

1. Ignore them when they say or do something that hurts my feelings.
2. Don't argue or fight with someone who is obviously not feeling good about him/herself.
3. Overlook it when someone is trying to tease me to get me mad.
4. Don't say things in anger – count to ten before I speak or don't say anything until the anger has passed.
5. Don't say negative things. I have a right to my opinions, but I do not have the right to express it.
6. Always try to think of everyone as doing the best they can – see everyone as the best that they can be.
7. Put myself in the other person's place and try to understand what their point-of-view is.
8. Treat others as I would like to be treated.

This is what I said/did that showed disrespect to my classmates:

_____

_____

_____

_____

I understand that one of the major expectations in this classroom is to respect others. I will work harder to abide by that policy in the future.

Please sign and date the bottom of your sheet before handing it in.

Adapted from the work of the Harden Middle School

TALKING LESSON

Directions: *Please copy this lesson onto a separate piece of paper. Be sure to title it "Talking Lesson" and put your name on the top right-hand corner of your paper. After you have completed the assignment, place this sheet and your paper in the box.*

I understand that time is one of the most valuable things we have. Forty or so minutes is so little time to do all the things we need to do in class, so it is vitally important to make every minute count. When I talk or mess or disrupt the class, I am wasting valuable learning time. That is not fair to my teacher, my classmates, or to myself.

I understand that it is okay to talk:

1. If I raise my hand and the teacher calls on me.

2. If talking is necessary to complete my assignment.

3. If it is free time and I have completed my assignments.

But I know that I must not talk:

1. When the teacher is talking.

2. When a student is asking or answering a question.

3. When the teacher has instructed the class to be quiet.

I understand that one of the major expectations in this classroom is to respect others. I will work harder to abide by that policy in the future.

Please sign and date the bottom of your sheet before turning it in.

Adapted from the work of the Harden Middle School

TIME OUT LESSON

Copy the lesson and fill in the blanks with your own words. Be sure to title it "Time-out Lesson" and put your name in the top right-hand corner of your sheet.

I understand that school is a place for learning. I understand that I choose how to use my time at school. I can get an education and learn more about myself and the world around me, or I can waste this time.

I understand that the teacher is responsible for many things. She needs to plan the lesson and then do everything possible to help students understand the material. The teacher has a big job because it is not easy to help a class full of students. When I behave disruptively, I am making it hard for the teacher to do her job. This isn't fair and I don't have the right to do this.

I understand that the other students in my class have a right to the best education possible. When I behave disruptively, I not only not only keep the teacher from doing her job, I am also keeping students from getting the best education possible. This is not fair and I don't have the right to do this.

I am here copying this because I was sent out of the room. I was sent out of the room because

_____

_____

_____

I understand that right now I am missing out on valuable learning time. Instead of learning, I am copying this lesson. I understand that I made a decision to behave unacceptably in class and the consequence for this was being sent out of the room. I understand that I have the power to make good decisions or bad decisions. When I make good decisions, I am rewarded. In school, this means getting a good education and feeling good about myself as a student. I understand that I deserve a good education and I have the power and responsibility to make this happen. When I return to class, I will

_____

_____

_____

_____

Adapted from the work of the Harden Middle School

POSTVENTION

_____'s BEHAVIOUR PLAN

EXPECTATIONS: _____ IS EXPECTED TO ALWAYS DO HIS BEST

He is also expected to achieve the following specific goals:

1. _____
2. _____
3. _____

The student and teacher have agreed to the following positive outcomes if _____ reaches his goals:

1. _____
2. _____
3. _____

The student will receive the following incentive(s):

_____

_____

_____

CONSEQUENCES

There will be consequences for serious unacceptable behaviour such as fighting, hitting, bullying or showing disrespect etc. as outlined in the school's Code of Behaviour. Sanctions will also be applied for failure to meet the expectations outlined above. Sanctions for failure to meet the specific targets will be:

1. _____
2. _____
3. _____

Other interventions applied with the plan will include:

1. _____
2. _____
3. _____

The plan will be monitored by the teacher, student, Principal and parents.
It will be reviewed in _____ weeks to assess the student's progress towards reaching his goals.

We have read and agree to the plan:

_____   _____
Student   Teacher

_____   _____
Parent   Principal/Deputy Principal

Date: _____

STUDENT MONITORING FORM

(FOR USE IN SUSPICION OF SUBSTANCE ABUSE/MISUSE)

STUDENT: _____   SUBJECT: _____

DATE: _____

Please tick observed pattern of behaviour:

ATTENDANCE & PUNCTUALITY/ WORK RATE	LATE	
	ABSENT	
	LOSS OF INTEREST IN SCHOOL WORK	
	DETERIORATION IN STANDARD OF WORK	
REQUESTS	FREQUENTLY ASKED TO GO TO THE TOILET	
	ASKED TO GO TO THE PHONE	
	OTHER	
BEHAVIOUR	INCOHERENT	
	CLUMSY	
	RESTLESS	
	AGGRESSIVE	
	AGITATED	
	TALKATIVE	
	FIGHTING	
	SUDDEN OUTBURSTS	
	OBSCENE GESTURES OR LANGUAGE	
	CONTINUALLY TIRED	
	OPENLY TALKING ABOUT SUBSTANCE USE (INCLUDING ALCOHOL)	
	ATTENTION SEEKING BEHAVIOUR	
	OTHER:	
PHYSICAL SYMPTOMS	DRY MOUTH	
	BLURRED VISION	
	NAUSEA	
	RUNNY NOSE	
	SCRATCHING	
	SPOTS OR SORES AROUND MOUTH OR NOSE	
	CHEST PAINS	
	CONFUSION	
	PIN SIZED PUPILS	
	SNEEZING	
	UNUSUAL/FREQUENT BRUISES OR SORES	
SMELLS	ALCOHOL	
	CIGARETTES	
	CANNABIS	
	SMELLS OF CHEMICALS	
	MOUTH FRESHENER	
HYGIENE	BAD HYGIENE	
	NO INTEREST IN PERSONAL APPEARANCE	
	DETERIORATION IN PERSONAL APPEARANCE	

Every School
Daily Progress Report

Today's Date _____

Teachers: _____ is to present this form to you for you feedback regarding his/her progress and behaviour in your class. Please respond when the student submits this form to you. Thank you.

Subject/ Teacher (teacher initial)	Prepared for Class?	Homework Assignment	On Time for Class?	Missing Assignments?	Today's Comment

Student Signature: _____

Parent Signature: _____

Student's To Do List for Today:

_____

_____

_____

_____

PUPIL SUPPORT CARD

Name: _____ Class: _____ Tutor: _____

Progress ☐ **Behaviour** ☐

Please use this card to comment on either the progress or behaviour (or both) of the student named above.

Progress: Please comment on standard of work, homework, attitude to work, punctuality, absenteeism, particular strengths or difficulties.

Behaviour: Please comment on all aspects of behaviour, positive or negative, where appropriate.

DATE	CLASS	PROGRESS/BEHAVIOUR	Teacher's Signature	Parent's Signature

YOU MAY PHOTOCOPY THIS PAGE

Behaviour Record

Student: _____ **Class:** _____

Date/Time	Behaviour Observed	Action Taken

SECTION
EIGHT

BIBLIOGRAPHY

References and
Useful Reading

References and Useful Reading

Albert, L. and Desisto, P. (1996) *Coooperative Discipline*. Minnesota: Circle Pines

Blum, P. (1998) *Surviving and Succeeding in Difficult Classrooms*. London: Routledge.

Boldt, S. (1998) *Showing the Way: Responses and approaches to the needs of students and early school leavers*. Dublin: Marino Institute of Education.

Canter, L. and Canter, M. (1992) *Assertive Discipline: Positive Behaviour Management for Today's Classroom*. California: Canter & associates Inc.

Charlton, T. and David, K. (Eds.) (1993) *Managing Misbehaviour in Schools*. (2nd ed.) London: Routledge.

Coloroso, B. (1995) *Kids are worth it! Giving your Child the Gift of Inner Discipline*. New York: William Morrow & Co. Inc.

Curwin, R.L. and Mendler, A.N. (1988) *Discipline with Dignity*. Alexandria: Association for Supervision and Curriculum Development.

Freiberg, H.J. (1998) Measuring School Climate: Let me Count the Ways, *Educational Leadership,* Vol. 56, No. 1, pp.22-26.

Glasser, W. (1990) *The Quality School: Managing Students Without Coercion*. New York: Perennial.

Goleman, D. (1995) *Emotional Intelligence* New York: Bantam.

Gootman, M.E. (1997) *The Caring Teacher's Guide to Discipline: Helping Young Students Learn Self-Control, Responsibility and Respect*. California: Corwin Press.

Gordon, D.T. (1999) Rising to the Discipline Challenge *Harvard Education Letter,* Vol. 15, No. 5, pp. 1-4.

Haberman, M. (1992) Creating Community Contexts That Educate: An Agenda for Improving education in Inner Cities in: Kaplan, L. (Ed) *Education and the Family*. Boston: Allyn and Bacon

Hansen, J.M. and Childs, J. (1998) Creating a School Where People Like to Be *Educational Leadership,* Vol. 56, No. 1, pp.14-17

Hewett, D. (Ed.) (1998) *Challenging Behaviour: Principles and Practices*. London: David Fulton Publishers.

Johnson, D. W., Johnson, R.T., Stevahn, L. and Hodne, P. (1997) The Three Cs of Safe Schools, *Educational Leadership,* Vol. 55, No. 2, pp.8-13.

Jones, F. (1987) *Positive Classroom Discipline*. New York: McGraw-Hill

Kavanagh, A.J. (1993) *Secondary Education in Ireland - Aspects of a Changing Paradigm*. Carlow: Patrician Brothers.

Kinder, K., Wilkin, A., Moor, H.Derrington, C. and Hogarth, S. (1999) *Raising Behaviour: A School View*. Berkshire: NFER-Nelson.

Klein, R. (1999) *Defying Disaffection: how schools are winning the hearts and minds of reluctant students*. Stoke-on-Trent: Trentham Books.

Kohn, A. (1996) *Beyond Discipline: From Compliance to Community*. Alexandria: ASCD

Lund, R. (1996) *A Whole School Behaviour Policy: A Practical Guide*. London: Kogan Page.

McGettrick, B.J. (1996) *Values in Education: Staff Development Day Handbook, Marino College*. Glasgow: St. Andrew's College.

McGrath, M. (1998) *The Art of Teaching Peacefully*. London: David Fulton Publishers.

McNamara, E. (1999) *Positive Pupil Management and Motivation: A Secondary Teacher's Guide*. London: David Fulton Publishers.

Martin, M. (1997) *Discipline in Schools: Report to the Minister for Education*. Dublin: DES

Mendler, A. N. (2001) *Connecting With Students*. Alexandria: Association for Supervision and Curriculum Development

Miller, A. (1996) *Pupil Behaviour and Teacher Culture* London: Cassell

Monahan, L. (1996) *Making School A Better Place* Dublin: Marino Institute of Education

Monahan, L. and Prendergast, N. (eds.) (1997) *Discipline and Stress: Beyond Control? Searching for Ways Forward* Dublin: Irish Association of Pastoral Care in Education.

Mosley, J. (1993) *Turn Your School Around.* Cambridgeshire: LDA

Munn, P., Johnstone, M. and Chalmers, V. (1992) *Effective Discipline in Secondary Schools and Classrooms.* London: Paul Chapman Publishers.

Newell, S. and Jeffery, D. (2002) *Behaviour Management in the Classroom: A Transactional Analysis Approach.* London: David Fulton Publishers.

O'Hara, J., Byrne, S.J. and McNamara, G. (2000) *Positive Discipline: An Irish Educational Appraisal and Practical Guide.* Dublin: The Greendale Project/DES/School of Education Studies, DCU.

O'Flynn, S. and Kennedy, H. (2000) *Conflict and Confrontation in the Classroom: Reflections on Current Practice.* Cork: Paradigm Press.

Rogers, B. (2000) *Behaviour Management: A Whole School Approach* London: Paul Chapman Publishing.

Rogers, B. (Ed.) (2002) *Teacher Leadership and Behaviour Management* London: Paul Chapman Publishing.

Rogers, C. and Freiberg, H.J. (1994) *Freedom to Learn.* (3rd ed.) New York: Macmillan.

Schreiber Dill, V. and Haberman, M. (1995) Building a Gentler School *Educational Leadership* Vol. 52, No. 5 Alexandria: Association for Supervision and Curriculum Development

Slee, R. (1995) *Changing Theories and Practices of Discipline.* London: Falmer Press.

Smith, A. (1996) *Discipline for Learning: A positive approach to teaching.*

Somerset: Discipline for Learning.

Starratt, R.J. (1995) *Leaders with Vision.* California: Corwin Press

Stone, L. (1990) *Managing Difficult Children in School.* Oxford: Blackwell.

Watkins, C. and Wagner, P. (1991) *School Discipline: a whole school approach.* (3rd ed.) Oxford: Blackwell.

Watkins, C. and Wagner, P. (2000) *Improving School Behaviour.* London: Paul Chapman Publishing.

Watkins, C. (2000) *Managing classroom behaviour: from research to diagnosis.* London: Instistute of Education, University of London.

NOTES

NOTES

NOTES

NOTES